INCULCATING ETHICS AND CITIZENSHIP BEHAVIOUR IN ISLAMIC FINANCIAL INSTITUTIONS:
The Issues and Consequences

INCULCATING ETHICS AND CITIZENSHIP BEHAVIOUR IN ISLAMIC FINANCIAL INSTITUTIONS:
The Issues and Consequences

Jihad Mohammad; Farzana Quoquab

PARTRIDGE

Print information available on the last page.

To order additional copies of this book, contact
Toll Free 800 101 2657 (Singapore)
Toll Free 1 800 81 7340 (Malaysia)
orders.singapore@partridgepublishing.com

www.partridgepublishing.com/singapore

About the Authors

Dr. Jihad Mohammad is a senior lecturer at International Business School, UTM, Malaysia. He has received his Dotorate degree from Universiti Kebangsaan Malaysia. He has presented papers at various international and national conferences and published articles in peer-reviewed international journals such as Asia Pacific Journal of Marketing and Logistics, International Journal of Business Governance and Ethics, Asian Academy of Management Journal, and Journal of Islamic Marketing. He has conducted workshops for postgraduate students regarding research methodology and structural equation modeling. His area of research interest includes organizational citizenship behaviour, psychological ownership, psychological capital, leadership, innovation, and Islamic work ethics.

Dr. Farzana Quoquab is a senior lecturer at International Business School, UTM. She has received her Doctorate degree from Universiti Kebangsaan Malaysia. She has presented papers at various international and national conferences and published articles in peer-reviewed international journals such as Asian Case Research Journal, Asia Pacific Journal of Marketing and Logistics, International Journal of Business Governance and Ethics, International Journal of Economics and Management, International Review of Management and Marketing, Pertanika Journal of Social Science and Humanities, Emerald Emerging Markets Case Studies, Asian Academy of Management Journal and Journal of Islamic Marketing. She is one of the editorial board members of 'Case Studies in Business and Management' and 'Journal of Economic and Administrative Science'.

Preface

All praise is for Allah (SWT); may He send peace and blessings on Prophet Muhammad, his family, and his companion.

The aim of this book is to highlight the phenomenon of ethic at workplace from Islamic standpoint. The concept of IWE has its origin in the holy Quran and the saying of Prophet Mohammad (saw). It stresses all good behaviors that can help the organization and its workforce to prosper and sustain into the future, and prohibits all bad deeds that can harm organization and its individuals. In spite of its importance, there is a paucity of research that has been devoted to study Islamic work ethic (IWE) and its impact on workplace outcome. Additionally, most of the research related to work ethics has been carried out in the Western country context and mostly from the view point of Protestant work ethics. However, there is a growing need to understand and discuss other work ethics from different religious perspectives.

Indeed, researchers have emphasized the crucial role of Islamic work ethic at workplace. It helps to regulate idividual and group behaviours, facilitates organizational development, and mobilizes the effectiveness and efficiency of organization and its individuals. Therefore, the main concern of this book is to undertand the role of Ismaic work ethic as predicotrs of workplace attitude and behavioir.

This book highlights the essentials about Islamic work ethics, organizational citizenship behaviour, and organizational justice for the success, prosperity, and sustainability of organization and it citizens. The book consists of five chapters. The first chapter discusses the notion of work ethic at workplace from Islamic perspective. In the second chapter; workplace attitudes and behaviour in term of citizenship behaviour and organizational justice are addressed. The third chapter provides an overview of Islamic banking industry in Malalysia. The fourth chapter addresses the existing gaps in the literature as well as in practice, and highlights the possible relationship between citizenship behaviour, organizational justice, and Islamic work ethics. Lastly, the fifth chapter provides practical contribution and suggestions for academicians and practitioners regarding how to inculcate Islamic work ethic at workplace.

Value of This Book

This book provides important theoretical and practical knowledge in the field of organizational behaviour. More specifically, this book provides understanding about organizational citizenship behaviour, organizational justice, and Islamic work ethic constructs in the context of Islamic banking industry in Malaysia. Additionally this book addresses the consequences of Islamic work ethics at the workplace.

This book contains verses of the Quran, saying of the prophet Muhammad (saw) and his companions. It also contains opinion of western and eastern thinkers and philosophers. This book is expected to provide managers of Islamic finanacial instituations with important information regading the role of Islamic work ethic in order to instil and practice it for the benefit of their organization. The book has derived some essential options for the decision makers at Islamic banks to effectively implement Islamic work ethic programs that can prevent their employees from workplace deviations.

Acknowledgement

First and foremost, we express humble appreciation to Allah the All-Mighty for guiding us and give us the strength, courage, and patience to complete this book. Also, we would like to thank the people who have provided us their time, guidance, support, valuable opinon, views, and feedback to know and learn more about citizenship behaviour, justice at workplace, and Islamic work ethic through their valuable publications.

A specific acknowledgment is due to specific individuals who have contributed to our knowledge and understanding regarding the subject matter of the book. They are Associate Professor Dr. Nik Mutasim Nik Abd. Rahman, Associate Professor Dr. Fazli Idris, Associate Professor Dr. Zafir Khan bin Mohd. Makhbul, Associate Professor Dr. Rosmah Mat Isa, Professor Dr. Arif Hassan, Professor Dr. June Poon, and Professor Ramayah.

Finally, we would like to express our deepest gratitude to our family members whose endless love and support given us the strength and confidence to finish this book; to our great parents Mr Mohammad Dahi Al Nusairt and Madam Sabha Mohammad Nusairat for their moral support, prayers, and encouragement; and to our brothers and sisters for their love and moral as well as spiritual support.

Jihad Mohammad
Farzana Quoquab

Ethics at Workplace: An Islamic Perspective

E thic is concerned with the nature of morality which attempts to define what is right or wrong, good or bad in relation to individuals' behaviour and decisions (Abd Rahman 2010; Hellriegel et al. 2001). Similarly, the World Book Encyclopaedia (1993) has defined this construct as a subdivision of philosophy that helps individuals to assess and decide on a particular course of moral conduct. In the same manner, Al-Ghazali (1982) defined ethic as the study of the beliefs of a specific religion, and to what extent actions are considered right or wrong for the purpose of practice from the point of view of that particular religion. Furthermore, Bateman and Snell (2002) defined ethic as a system of rules governing the ordering of values. Subsequently, ethic can be defined as a philosophical branch which attempt to define what is morally good and bad, right and wrong in human behaviour.

At workplace ethic, refers to employees' work related beliefs and values which shape their moral aspect such as intention to work diligently and to be committed to their work (Shamsudin et al. 2010). The concept of work ethic is synonymous with work values and therefore employees' ethical values are similar to their work values (Hitt 1990). Moreover, it goes beyond individual preferences and emphasizes certain aspects of moral values over others (Hofstede 1999). Work ethics contribute positively to organizational performance and its productivity (Noe et al. 2000), reduce absenteeism, counterproductive behaviours, and employee turnover (Sheehy 1990). Consequently, it plays a crucial role in mobilizing a nation's economic success or failure (Furnham 1990). Hence, the work ethic construct has been given significant research attentions and research in this field is still growing (see Ali 2005; Ali & Al-Owaihan 2008; Yunus et al. 2011).

According to Al-Modaf (2005), work ethic is indispensable for any organization to function, prosper, and survive in the future. Additionally, Abeng (1997) indicated that organizations could function more effectively and efficiently by adopting an ethical framework that guide and help to organize their work. Work ethic also contributes toward economic development (Congleton 1991); it accelerates the success of an organization and its employees (Yunus et al. 2011). Research has shown that belief in work ethic is highly predictive of work related behaviours and outcomes (Furnham 1990), such as performance (Andrisani & Parnes 1983), interest in challenging and non-routine task (Bahagat 1979), satisfaction (Blood 1969), occupational accomplishment and career mobility (Andrisani 1978), and organizational commitment (Oliver 1990). In other words, work ethic is believed to reflect an individual's disposition toward various aspects of his work, including preference for work involvement (Randall & Cote 1991) and attitude toward monetary and non-monetary rewards (Cherrington 1980). On the other hand, a decline in work ethic could have negative impact on organization's productivity (Yandle 1992) and might encourage absenteeism and cause a high rate of turnover (Shimko 1992). Thus, individuals' ability to meet organization's needs depends largely on their identification with work values (Abu-Saad 2003).

Ali and Al-Kazemi (2007), argued that work ethic may differ across time span and culture. Some of the influential work ethic are: (i) PWE which has shaped western society's work values such as work creativity, commitment, dedication to work, and avoiding unethical methods of wealth accumulation (Brief & Aldag 1994); (ii) Confucian work ethic which has its influence on the Japanese and Chinese work values, such as hard work, respect for time, loyalty, dedication, and social order (Coate 1987); and (iii) IWE which has shaped the Muslim societies' work values such as hard work, cooperation, dedication, consultation, creativity and social relation (Ahmad 1976; Ali 1988;Kamaluddin & Manan 2010; Kumar & Rose 2009).

ETHIC FROM RELIGIOUS VIEW POINT

The Encyclopaedia of World Religions (1998) defined ethic as the right behavioural conducts that are guided by one's religion. All religions have their own set of ethical principles which guide their followers regarding the *do's* and *don'ts* (Abbasi et al. 2011; Yunus et al. 2011). Typically, all religions share some similarities such as enjoining justice, generosity, forgiveness, and patience while at the same time refraining from stealing, vandalism, and exploitation (Abd Rahman 2010). A discussion on work ethic from two different standpoints i.e., Islam and Christianity, as well as major similarities and differences between these two views are briefly discussed.

The notion of IWE originated from the holy *Quran* and the sayings and practice of Prophet Muhammad (saw) (Ali 1988, Yousef 2000b). According to Muhammad (saw), "Hard work causes sins to be absolved and that no one eat better food than that which he eats out of his work" (Yousef 2001: 153). The holy *Quran* motivates individuals to attain necessary skills and abilities, and praises those who work hard to earn a living (Yousef 2001). Moreover, IWE perceives work as a virtue which helps individuals to find a balance between their personal life and their social life (Ali 2005). Additionally, while the Christian and Jewish religious faith views the need for work as a consequence of human sin (Lipset 1990), IWE holds a positive outlook toward work (Abu-Saad 2003).

The notion of PWE was introduced and advanced by Weber, a German scholar, in 1958. According to Weber, Protestant ethic has played a major role in the development of economy; it has greatly influence the development of capitalism in western countries. Specifically, Weber related the success achieved by western countries to religious factors (Yousef 2001). He postulated that the PWE had spiritual orientation toward capitalism and relied upon the assumption that work and financial success were ways to accomplish personal and religious goals (Kidron 1978). Moreover, PWE played a major role in changing the attitudes and behaviours of Western society toward work, one from disdain to admiration (Ali & Al-Kazemi 2007).

In general, both ethic systems agreed on categorizing actions and conducts into two main groups of good and bad or right and wrong. Furthermore, both systems considered behaviours that conform to their teaching and principles as good, and those that go against their rules and regulations as bad. Additionally, they commanded their followers to follow good behaviour and avoid bad deeds to achieve targeted goals. Those who abide by the precepts of ethical systems are deemed as deserving respect and trustworthy, whereas those who go against their ethical systems are considered as bad citizens. At the workplace, IWE and PWE place great important on hard work, commitment to work, creativity and innovativeness, cooperation and consultation to overcome conflict, and avoiding illegal methods of gathering wealth (Yousef 2001).

Nonetheless, IWE is different from PWE in several aspects. First, Christianity became secular (i.e. separating religion from daily life action and activities) and as a result PWE became more focused on the material aspect of work; Islam, on the other hand, never separate religion from life and thus IWE is more oriented toward creating equilibrium at the workplace by focusing on the spiritual side of work as well as the materialistic aspect (Wan Norhasniah Wan Husin 2012). Moreover, Islam considers work as an act of worship and is strongly tied to the *Quran* and the instructions of *Sunnah*, whereas PWE is not tied to religious teaching. For instance, interest rate which is absolutely prohibited by IWE is considered as the basic pillar of Western society (Wan Norhasniah Wan Husin 2012). Moreover, unlike PWE, IWE gives more emphasize to intention rather than result. For example Prophet Mumhammad (saw) stated "Actions are recorded according to intention, and man will be rewarded or punished accordingly". Additionally, IWE considers engagement in economic activities as compulsory for every capable individual, which is not the case of PWE (Ali 1988; Yousef 2001).

The focus of this book is IWE, hence the following sections will discusses ethic from Islamic perspective, Islam and its main sources, and the value of work in Islam. Finally, the concept of IWE is elaborated.

Ethic from Islamic Perspective

Islam has instituted its own principles of ethical system in every aspect of human life, such as physical, spiritual, and intellectual, as well as in business and work related issues (Abd Rahman 2010; Ahmad 2011; Rice 1999). Islam has established the basis for *halal* (permissible) and *haram* (prohibited), good and bad behaviour, and right and wrong conducts. These Islamic codes of conducts originated from the holy *Quran* and the *Sunnah* (Zulkifli Muhammad et al., 2008); these codes explain and guide the relationship between man and Allah (SWT), between individuals and their subordinates, and between individuals and other creatures in the universe (Zulkifli Muhammad et al. 2008; Tinker 2004). Both sources (*Quran* and *Sunnah*) consider ethic as the main objective of Islam (Zaroug 1999). The holy *Quran* says: "We sent you not but as mercy for all creatures" (21: 107). The Prophet (saw) said, "I was sent to complete morals" (narrated by al-Bukhari in al-adab al-mufrad).

According to Ali (1988), the Islamic code of conduct which deals with the ethical aspects of working in an organization is referred to IWE. This concept emphasizes on truthfulness, honesty, proficiency, sincerity, and fairness in organizations (Al-Modaf 2005). In addition, IWE stresses collaboration, consultation, equity, unity, and spirituality at work place (Youef 2001). Therefore, practicing IWE in an organization would enhance employees' honesty, trust, and creativity (Dannhauser 2007).

Islam and Its Main Sources

The word Islam is Arabic word which means *submission*, *surrender*, and *obedience* to Allah the Almighty (SWT) (Khurshid Ahmad 2002). It is a social constitution which guides Muslims in their worship to Allah the Creator, and in their conduct with one another as well as with other creatures (Zulkifli Muhammad et al. 2008; Tinker 2004). As a religion, Islam stands for belief in Allah (SWT), in all prophets, and in the last messenger, Muhammad (saw). It is a complete and comprehensive way of conduct for the human life (Ali 1998; Al-A'ali 2008) and govern the entire socio-economic system (Khraim 1999) – physical, spiritual, social, financial, economic, etc. (Abdel Rahman Ahmad Abdel Rahman1995; Askari & Taghavi 2005; Ahmad 2011).

According to Kamaluddin and Manan (2010), the Islamic value system comprises of three main fundamental teachings. The first is *aqidah* or strong belief in the Oneness of Allah (SWT). The second is *ibadah* or one's submission and obedience to Allah (SWT), while the third is *akhlaqh* which captures the concept of Islamic work related values (Beekun & Rafik Isa 1998). Islamic value system stresses on harmony, cooperation, forgiveness, kindness, and brotherhood (Atiyah 1999; Khalil & Abu Saad 2009). Moreover, it encourages proficiency and efficiency (*Ihsan*); sincerity (*ikhlas*), passion for excellence (*al-falah*), constant mindfulness of the Almighty; piety (*taqwa*), truthfulness (*amanah*), patience (*sabar*), moderation, dependability, gratefulness, consistency, and discipline (Albahi & Ghazali 1994). In a nutshell, the Islamic value system is guided by the *Quran* and *Sunnah* which emphasize on values which are useful and guide mankind to the right direction.

The Holy Quran

Ushama (1998: 18), an Islamic scholar, has clearly explained the Holly *Quran* by stating that,

> "The *Quran* is the miraculous, inimitable, indestructible, preserved, and infallible word of Allah (SWT), revealed to Muhammad (saw), the last of the prophets and messengers. It was revealed through the archangel *Jibril*, preserved in *al-masahif*, transmitted to us gradually; and by *mutawatir*, is regard as an act of devotion (*ibadah*) upon recitation, beginning with the opening entitled *suratal-Fatihah* and concluding with *surat al-Nas*".

It is a source of knowledge which provides important facts and explanations (Mohsen 2007). In this Holly Book, Allah (SWT) declared that *Quran* is the major source of Knowledge.

"To thee a Book explaining All things, a guide, a Mercy, And Glad Tiding to Muslims". (*Quran* 16:89; translated by Ali 1987).

This knowledge and guidance also provides the fundamental of IWE. Some of the IWE concepts (e.g., hard work, patience, continuous improvement) that originate from the Islamic principles are discussed below in brief.

Hard work is a major element in IWE. Allah (SWT) rewards those who believe in Him and His teachings, and those who work honestly and truthfully

(*Quran* 2:62; translated by Ali 1987). In another verse, the *Quran* states that those who are faithful and work with honesty, fairness, and justice shall enter heaven (*Quran* 2:82; translated by Ali 1987). Furthermore, it is suggested that, one should do a work that is within his ability and not make promises that he cannot keep (*Quran* 6:135; translated by Ali 1987).

Patience is another component of IWE. The Holy *Quran* stresses the benefits of being patient by stated that those who are patient, stable, loyal, and work in a righteous way will be pardoned, and in return they will be rewarded (*Quran* 11:11; translated by Ali 1987).

Continuous improvement also reflects some aspect of IWE. Islam highlights the importance of continuous improvement and this is also stated in the Holly *Quran*. For example, it is mentioned that believers who do their work with righteousness and to the full extent of their ability shall enter Heaven (*Quran* 7: 42; translated by Ali 1987).

The Sunnah

Sunnah literally means the path or the way of Prophet Muhammad (saw), and comprises his saying, actions, deeds, and utterances (Al-Buraey 1990). It consists of thousands of *Hadith*, commendations of certain actions upon various occasions, explanations of various phenomena, and approval or disapproval, or both, of the deeds of those around him (Al-Buraey 1990).

According to the Islamic faith, Prophet Muhammad (saw) was an example of an individual who was upright, merciful, truthful, brave, generous, the best teacher and preacher, and he refrained from evil in all his dealings and actions (Esposito 2005). He (saw) implemented laws and emphasized fairness as the foundation of both spiritual and worldly success (Ali 2005). He (saw) emphasized hard work by stating that it is one way of earning forgiveness for one's sins and, therefore, one should try to earn his/her own wages through hard work (Ali 2005).

Value of Work in Islam

Islam perceives work as an *Ibadah* (religious duty) and *Jihad* for the sake of Allah (SWT). In Islam, work is viewed as a sincere and dedicated effort that drives individuals to obtain benefit for themselves, for others and for society as a whole (Gibbs et al. 2007; Khalil & Abu-Saad 2009). Therefore, the Holly *Quran* fervently suggests that individuals to work, since work determines the true value of their existence. In reflecting this view, the holy *Quran* states that all prophets worked during their life time. The holy Book states that, "He [Allah] has also made subservient to you all that is in the heavens and earth" (*Quran* 45: 13). Additionally, in Islam, work is ranked as a superior form of worship. As such, Prophet Muhammad (saw) stated that: "Worship of the Creator (SWT) has seventy parts, the best of which is solvent business" (Ali & Al-Owaihan 2008: 11). In support of this view, Ibn Kaldun (1989: 273), the medieval Arab sociologist, mentioned that engaging in work and business activities can achieve four objectives: "Enhance collaboration and mutual understanding among people, satisfy the needs of people, increase wealth, and prompt the development of cities".

Due to its spiritual and earthly importance, several researchers have discussed the notion and importance of *work* from the Islamic perspective (see Abeng 1997; Bashir 1998). Ali and Al-Owaihan (2008) suggested that, at the organizational level, IWE could contribute positively to organization's performance and prosperity. Abeng (1997) also indicated that IWE is one of the measures to improve work performance amongst Muslims. Additionally Abuznaid (2009) mentioned that IWE could affect the ethical behaviours of Muslims in an organization in various ways, such as preventing corruption and abuse of power, abstaining from cheating and deceit, and taking care of employees and their rights, which in turn would enhance effectiveness, efficiency, integrity, and better quality.

Since Islam stresses the importance of 'work' as well as the 'quality of the work' (*itqan*), it is every Muslim's responsibility to work hard. Prophet Muhammad (saw) highlighted two aspects of successful work: quality and quantity. He (saw) stated that, "Allah blesses a person who perfects his craft" and "Allah loves a person who learns precisely how to perform his work and does it right" (Ali & Al-Owaihan 2008: 11). Likewise, Muhammad (saw) said "The best work is the one that results in benefit" and "The best of people are those who benefit others". Moreover, Islam views work as a source of psychological and social gratifications. Allah (SWT) emphasizes the value of work by linking work to the worship of Him (SWT) in this verse of the Quran, "And when the prayer is finished, then may ye disperse through the land, and seek of the bounty of Allah" (*Quran* 62: 10). Moreover, engaging in economic activities is obligatory upon Muslims (Ali 1988). Additionally, Ali (1992) alluded to what Ali (*ra*), the fourth successor, said, "Persist in your action with a noble end in mind... failure to perfect your work while you are sure of the reward is injustice to yourself" (Ali 1992: 507).

In emphasizing the value of work, Ikhwan-us-Safa (1999) mentioned the benefits of engaging in work as a way to reduce poverty, attain good manners and important skills, gain knowledge, and reach salvation. It is obvious that unemployment posed serious threat to both individuals and nation as a whole since it increases crime rate and violence such as drug addiction, robbery, vandalism, embezzlement, etc. (Lafree 1999). Considering these circumstances, the holy *Quran* instructs the Muslims to shun laziness, wasting time and unproductive activities (Abeng 1997). Moreover, Islam forbids hoarding and gambling which represent a situation of not working (Al-Jazairy 1988; Assamalloty 1998). As such, Islam encourages the act of entrepreneurship (Al-Modaf 2005). Hence, we can conclude that Islam emphasizes the importance of work as a way to protect, develop and nurture society and help citizens to achieve respect, honour, and dignity.

Accordingly, the *Sunnah* of Prophet Muhammad (saw) considers work as extremely valuable. He (saw) preached that, "Honest and trustworthy merchant will be with the prophets, the truthful and martyrs" (At-Tirmidhi). To emphasize the importance of work, the Holly *Quran* mentions work in more than 50 different verses (Abeng 1997). Moreover, Prophet Muhammad (saw) said, he first command of Allah (SWT) to Adam (pbuh) after the fall of the land is work to plant the earth with his hands and takes advantage of his earning. The Prophet's (saw) commanded individuals to work hard and to be productive even at the last moment of one's life. For example, one man came to the Prophet (saw) and asked for charity. Instead, the Prophet gave the man an axe and a rope and said "One would rather take a rope and cut wood and carry it than ask others" (Az-Zubaidi 1996: 749). This moral of the story is that the Prophet (saw) wanted to establish a role and build a generation of entrepreneurs through empowerment, not through giving.

In a nutshell, Islam highly values productive and fruitful work, and gives emphasis to *Halal* work that does not contradict the *Shariah* principles. Islam perceives work as the highest form of worship (*Ibadah*) of Allah (SWT). Moreover, Islam emphasizes on hard work to achieve high quality. Additionally, Islam considers work as compulsory as a way for individuals and groups to achieve a respected life regardless of their status in society. Islam also urges Muslims to continue working till the last day of their lives as a way of gaining knowledge and enhancing skills, abilities and capabilities.

At workplace IWE advocates honesty, flexibility, fairness, generosity, and responsibility (Abbasi et al. 2011; Yousef 2001). In addition, it encourages individuals to acquire the skills and technology needed to achieve excellence and continuously improve performance (Yousef 2000a). Additionally, IWE emphasizes cooperation and consultation at the workplace as a way to overcome barriers and avoid mistakes (Naresh Kumar & Raduan Che Rose 2009). In addition, IWE also encourages social relations at work to help meet ones' need and establish equilibrium in one's personal and social life (Yousef 2001). On the other hand, not working hard is considered as a source of failure in life (Ali 1988). Additionally, IWE views work not as an end in itself, but as a means to advance personal growth and social relations (Naresh Kumar & Raduan Che Rose 2009). In brief, IWE argues that life without hard work has no meaning and engagement in economic activities is an obligation (Yousef 2001).

Workplace Attitude and Behaviour

Although the relationships between IWE and individual as well as organizational variables are investigated (see Ali & Al-Kazemi 2007; Khalil & Saad, 2009; Khan et al. 2013) the direct and indirect relationships between IWE and variables like organizational citizenship behavior (OCB), and perceived organizational justice (POJ) are yet to be examined. Past studies found that OCB, POJ, can have substantial effect on effectiveness, efficiency and success of organization and can determine organization's ability to survive and sustain into the future (Cropanzano et al. 2009; Greenberg and Colquitt 2005; Podaskoff et al. 2009). Therefore, the focus of this book is to understand these constructs and its relationship with IWE.

ORGANIZATIONAL CITIZENSHIP BEHAVIOUR

The study of organizational citizenship behaviour has appeared as an important topic in the field of organizational psychology, human resource management, and organizational behaviour. Since its inception, OCB has received considerable research interest due to its contribution to organizational effectiveness (Farh et al. 1997; Podaskoff & Mackenzie 1997; Podaskoff et al. 1997), organization's survival (Organ 1988a), organization's function (Podaskoff et al. 2000), organization's sustainability (Lin et al. 2010), and the well-being of individuals, groups, organizations as well as the society in general (Penner et al. 2005). Therefore, it has been increasingly attracting the interests of both academicians and practitioners (LePine et al. 2002; Motowidlo et al. 1997; Organ & Rayan 1995).

Altough different authors have defined OCB in different ways, in general it implies "The functional, extra-role, pro-social behaviours that is directed toward individuals, groups and the organization" (Schnake 1991: 738). According to Farh et al. (1997), the concept, nature, and measures of OCB has been developed from three sources: (i) Katz's taxonomy, which includes helping fellow members and being innovative and spontaneous at the workplace; (ii) Smith et al's (1983) work which yielded two major dimensions i.e., altruism and compliance; and (iii) the classic Greek philosophy which focuses on loyalty and cooperation as significant forms of OCB (Van Dyne et al. 1994). However, the most cited conceptualization of OCB is perhaps from Organ's (1988a: 4) work, in which OCB reflects individual behaviour that is "Neither described nor prescribed by organization, hence, cannot be directly recognized by the formal reward system and that in aggregate promote the effective functioning of the organization".

Importance of Organizational Citizenship Behaviour

A meta-analysis review indicated that OCB is significantly associated with employees' productivity and efficiency as well as customer satisfaction (Podaskoff et al. 2009). Moreover, Hoffman et al. (2007) emphasized a positive association between extra role behaviour and task performance. In general, OCB has a direct effect on organization's efficiency and profitability, innovation and process development, and customer satisfaction and retention (Shweta & Jha 2009). Therefore, scholars and managers have been showing increasing interests in employees' contribution toward organization that surpasses their official work requirements (Grant & Mayer 2009; Hoffman et al. 2007; Podaskoff et al. 2009).

As a whole, past research suggested that OCB contributes to organizational success in several ways; OCB (a) improves coworker and managerial output (Mackenzie et al. 1991, 1993; Organ 1988a, 1988b; Podaskoff & Mackenzie 1992, 1994), (b) helps coordinate activities within and across work groups (Karambayya 1990; Smith et al. 1983), (c) increase organization's ability to attract and retain talented employees (George & Bettenhausen 1990; Organ 1988a, 1988b; Podaskoff et al. 2000), (d) enhances the stability of organizational performance, which permits managers to blueprint and allocate rare resources effectively (Podaskoff et al. 2000), and (e) enables organizations to cope with and compete in aggressive environments (Podaskoff & Mackenzie 1997; Podaskoff et al. 2000).

These myriad of benefits of OCB to organizational prosperity and success have led the research interests to identify its antecedents and consequences. This book represents one of such effort.

Conceptualization of Organizational Citizenship Behaviour

Since its inception, different authors have defined OCB in different ways (Table 1). At the early stage of conceptualization of this construct, Smith et al. (1983) perceived it as the combination of 'helping' and 'compliance' behaviour. In a later study, Organ (1988a: 4) modified and elaborated the definition of OCB by stating that OCB is the "behaviour from individuals' side that is discretionary, not directly or explicitly acknowledged by the official reward and/or punishment system, and that over time and across people promote the effective functioning of organization". By discretionary Organ was referring to specific behaviour that is not imposed by organizations or is a prerequisite of a job description, but is a matter of individual choice, and thus, its omission is not subject to punishment (Rego & Cunha 2010). Organ (1997) modified the definition and stated that OCB is a performance that helps maintain and enhance the social and psychological aspect of an organization and, thus support task performance. In a more recent work, Organ et al. (2006) stressed the discretionary nature of OCB by defining it as discretionary behaviour that exceeds employees' role requirement and cannot be recognized by organization's formal system. In support of this view researchers have conceptualized OCB as a multidimensional construct that is functional, extra-role, pro-social organizational behaviour, discretionary in nature, directed toward specific individual, groups and/or the whole organization, that is neither prescribed officially by the organization, nor is there any direct rewards or punishments (Krishnan & Arora 2008; Lovell et al. 1999; Schnake 1991; Williams & Anderson 1991). According to Chu et al. (2005), this definition includes three main features of OCB: (i) the behaviour must be voluntary, (ii) it is multidimensional in nature, and (iii) it is aggregated over time and persons.

Table 1 Definitions and dimensions of OCB in selected past studies (organized on the basis of year)

Author and year	Definitions	Dimensions
Bateman and Organ (1983); Smith et al. (1983)	Discretionary behaviour that exceeds formal role and aim to assist other employees in the organization.	Altruism and generalized compliance.
Organ (1988a: 4)	OCB is "behaviour from individuals' side that is discretionary, not directly or explicitly acknowledged by the official reward and/or punishment system, and that over time and across people promote the effective functioning of organization".	Altruism, civic virtue, conscientiousness, courtesy, and sportsmanship.
Williams and Anderson (1991)	OCB refers to set of behaviour demonstrated by a workforce that is considered as extra-role, or discretionary in nature, and thus not defined or rewarded by the organization's official system.	OCBO and OCBI.
Borman and Motowidlo (1993)	OCB refers to behaviour that supports the organizational, social, and psychological environment that serve as facilitator for tasks to be accomplished.	Voluntary behaviour, persistence in completing tasks; helping behaviour, abide by organization's rules and procedures, defend organization's objectives.
Van Dyne et al. (1994)	OCB is a multidimensional concept which consists of all behaviours that are considered positive and relevant, including in-role behaviour, extra-role behaviour and political behaviour.	Obedience, loyalty, and participation.
Organ (1997)	Performance that contribute to the maintenance and enhancement of social and psychological context that support task performance.	Helping, courtesy, and conscientiousness.

Organ and Paine (1999	Followed Organ's (1988) definition.	Altruism and general compliance.
Lovell et al. (1999)	OCB refers to activities that employees engaged in which exceed basic job requirements set by organizations and support the welfare of co-workers, work groups, or the organization.	Altruism, sportsmanship, and mediation.
Podaskoff et al. (2000)	Followed Organ's (1988) definition.	Helping behaviour, sportsmanship, organizational loyalty, organizational compliance, individual imitative, civic virtue and self-development.
Rotundo and Sackett (2002)	OCB is individual behaviour that promotes the goal of an organization by contributing to its social and psychological environment.	Uni-dimensional.
Lee and Allen (2002)	OCB is employee's behaviour that, although not critical to the task or job, serves to facilitate organizational functioning.	OCBI and OCBO.
LePine et al. (2002)	Followed Organ's (1988) definition.	OCBI and OCBO
Organ et al. (2006)	Discretionary behaviour that exceeds employees' role requirement and cannot be recognized by the organizational formal punishment or reward system.	Helping, civic virtue, organizational loyalty, organizational compliance, sportsmanship, and individual initiative.
Podaskoff et al. (2009)	Followed Williams and Anderson's (1991) definition.	OCBI and OCBO.

Source: Compiled by the authors

In a similar manner, Van Dyne et al. (1994) defined OCB as a multidimensional concept that consists of all behaviour that are considered as positive and relevant. Such behaviour includes in-role behaviour, extra-role behaviour, and political behaviour. These behaviours stem from the intention to benefit individual, group, or organization as a whole. Additionally, Borman and Motowidlo (1993) and Rotundo and Sackett (2002) perceived OCB as behaviour that support organizational, social, and psychological environment which in turn facilitate the accomplishment of tasks. In other words, it refers to a set of behaviour that supports organizational culture and climate. Such behaviour includes accomplishing tasks and activities that are not officially part of the job, assisting others on the job, and defending organizational goals (Borman & Motowidlo 1993).

However, the definition of OCB depends on (i) distinguishing it from the in-role behaviour, (ii) differentiating it from other similar concepts, and (iii) understanding its dimensionality. Therefore, the next few paragraphs will discuss these three main issues pertaining to OCB to operationalize it for the present study.

Distinguishing In-Role Behaviour from Extra-Role Behaviour

Nearly a half century ago, Katz (1964) identified extra-role behaviour as one of the three major behaviours which are essential for any organizations to achieve their goals and to become more effective and competitive in their environments. Two other behaviours are organizational commitment and employee's in–role performance. In general, employees' performance consists of both in-role and extra-role behaviour (Williams & Anderson 1991). Therefore, it is crucial to distinguish between in-role and extra-role behaviour for three basic reasons. *First*, empirical evidence revealed that, in evaluating employees' overall performances, managers take into consideration employees' extra-role behaviour as well as in-role behaviour (see Borman & Motowidlo 1993; MacKenzie et al. 1991, 1993; Podaskoff, MacKenzie & Hui 1993). *Second*, both types of behaviours have been proven to have important effect on individual and organizational performances (George & Bettenhausen 1990; Podaskoff & MacKenzie 1992, 1994, 1997; Walz & Niehoff 1996). *Third*, both types of performances have been proven to have different antecedents and consequences (Organ 1988a, 1988b, 1990). For example, empirical evidence suggests that in-role performance is likely to be an antecedent of job satisfaction (Bagozzi 1980; Wanous 1974) but extra-role behaviour is likely to be the consequence of it (Organ 1988a, 1988b, 1990).

The purpose of differentiating in-role from extra-role behaviour is to draw a distinction between the types of behaviours that an employee is expected to perform according to official employment contract (in-role behaviour) and those behaviours that surpass main job related responsibilities (extra-role behaviour) (Koster & Sanders 2006). However, Organ's (1988a, 1988b) conceptualization of OCB strongly suggests considering OCB as an extra-role behaviour, rather than in-role behaviour, as this definition stresses that OCB goes beyond formal job responsibilities and duties. Conversely, Van Dyne et al. (1994) did not distinguish between in-role and extra-role behaviour. They proposed considering OCB as a combination of both extra and in–role behaviours. They categorized all positive and relevant types of behaviour performed by employees in organizations as OCB.

Morgeson (1999) contended that the distinction between in-role and extra-role is based on job occupants, types of organization, and time span. Moreover, Morrison (1994) argued that OCB varies based on differences among employees as well as supervisors. She noted that different employees perceive in-role and extra-role behaviour in different ways. Morrison (1994) claimed that employees' motivation to engage in OCB is due to the fact that these behaviours are viewed as a part of individual's job, whereas Pond et al. (1997) emphasized that employees engage in OCB as these behaviours are perceived as being directly rewarded.

Organ (1990) drew a distinction between in-role and extra-role behaviour by stating that in-role behaviour is motivated by economic exchange, whereas extra-role behaviour is driven by social exchange. Besides, in distinguishing extra-role from in-role behaviour, Van Dyne et al. (1995) defined in-role behaviour as behaviour that is required in order to perform the main duties and responsibilities assigned based on official contract with the employer, whereas extra-role behaviour is discretionary behaviour that benefits the organization and that exceed main job duties. Farh et al. (2004) differentiated OCB from task performance by stating that OCB is an individual's conscious and spontaneous choice of going the extra mile rather than being confined within the fixed job requirements; it can be measured by using attitudinal and dispositional measures instead of technical task performance; it also outperforms in social, psychological and political context compared to the technical context. Borman

(2004) further revealed two important distinctions between task performance and citizenship performance. *First*, task activities usually differ based on the types of job, but activities concerning citizenship are mostly similar across jobs. *Second*, the level of task performance can be anticipated by individual's knowledge, skills, and abilities, whereas citizenship performance depends on individual's predisposition.

From the above discussion, it is evident that in-role behaviour differs greatly from extra-role behaviour. In-role behaviour includes employee's behaviour that helps organizations perform their contractual and official activities, whereas extra-role behaviour includes employees' activities that exceed their job description Colquitt et al. (2009). This fact is supported by numerous past studies (see Mackenzie et al. 1991; McNeely & Meglino 1994; Motowidlo & Van Scotter 1994; Motowidlo & Schmit 1999; Motowidlo et al. 1997; Organ 1988a, 1988b, 1990; Van Dyne & LePine 1998; Williams & Anderson 1991).

Differentiating Organizational Citizenship Behaviour from Similar Concepts

There is little consensus among organizational behaviour scholars in labelling OCB. In past literature, terminologies used in the domains of behaviour that overlap with OCB include *prosocial organizational behaviour* (Brief & Motowidlo 1986; George 1990, 1991; George & Bettenhause 1990), *organizational spontaneity* (George & Brief 1992; George & Jones 1997), *extra-role behaviour* (Van Dyne et al. 1995), and *contextual performance* (Borman & Motowidlo 1993). Although these terminologies differ from one another in some important aspect, they all highlight behaviour that involves cooperation and helping others in an organization (Motowidlo & Van Scotter 1994). Additionally, they are not mentioned explicitly in employees' official employment contract but are necessary for the successful operation of an organization (Korsgaard et al. 2010). The similarities and differences between OCB and its similar concepts are summarized in Table 2.

Table 2 Similarities and differences between
OCB and similar concepts in several
selected past studies

Construct	Similarities	Differences
Contextual performance (CP)	• OCB and CP reflect cooperation and helping behaviour inside an organization (Motowidlo & Van Scotter 1994).	• CP is not considered as extra-role behaviour; on the other hand OCB is considered as extra-role behaviour (Organ 1997). • Contextual performance is recognized by the formal reward system, whereas OCB is not recognized by this system (Organ 1997).
Prosocial organizational behavior (POB)	• OCB and POB capture cooperation and helping behaviour within organization (Motowidlo & Van Scotter 1994). • Both are not mentioned formally in official employment contract (Korsgaard et al. 2010).	• POB includes in-role and extra role behaviour (Brief & Motowidlo 1986), whereas OCB includes only extra-role behaviour (Organ 1988a, 1988 b). • POB encompasses functional and dysfunctional behaviours (Brief & Motowidlo 1986), whereas OCB subsumes functional behaviour (Organ 1988a, 1988 b).
Organizational spontaneity behaviour (OSB)	• OCB and OSB indicate cooperation behaviour at workplace (Motowidlo & Van Scotter 1994). • Both are not recognized by the explicit employment contract (Korsgaard et al. 2010).	• OSB includes behaviour which is officially rewarded by organization (George & Brief 1992), whereas OCB is not recognized by the formal reward system (Organ 1988a, 1988 b).
Extra-Role Behaviour (ERB)	• OCB and ERB denote helping behaviour in an organization (Motowidlo &Van Scotter 1994). • Both are not clearly acknowledged in formal employment contract (Korsgaard et al. 2010).	• ERB includes two concepts that are not part of OCB, i.e., whistle blowing and principled organizational dissent (Organ et al. 2006).

Source: Compiled by the authors

Contextual performance (CP) is the closest concept to OCB which is parallely used in literature (Borman & Motowidlo 1993). Borman and Motowidlo defined it as behaviour that supports organizational, social, and psychological environments. They identified five different categories of CP: performing of tasks beyond a person's formal job requirement, following organization's rules and regulations, diligence in handling and coping with important task requirements, helping others, and protecting organization's objectives. These five categories are similar to Organ's (1988a) five dimensions of OCB, i.e., altruism, general compliance, sportsmanship, civic virtue, and courtesy (Organ 1997). However, OCB is different from CP in different aspect. For example, CP can be recognized by a formal reward system, which is not the case in OCB, and CP does not require that the behaviour be extra-role (Organ 1997).

Brief and Motowidlo (1986) perceived prosocial organizational behaviour (POB) as individual's activities that are directed to benefit co-workers, group and/or the whole organization. Additionally, Brief and Motowidlo stated that these behaviours were either in-role or extra-role behaviour and could be organizational functional or dysfunctional. *Functional* extra-role behaviour consists of behaviours such as helping others, defending organizations from unpredicted risk, and suggesting organizational developments (Katz 1964). *Dysfunctional* extra-role behaviour might include helping co-worker in ways that benefit them personally but is harmful to the organization (Brief & Motowidlo 1986). These behaviours are similar to OCB with the exclusion of certain dysfunctional behaviours. However, these dysfunctional behaviours create confusion and have led to POB as a construct to fall out of favour with number of researchers (LePine et al. 2002; Podaskoff et al. 2000).

In a similar vein, George and Brief (1992) proposed the 'organizational spontaneity behaviours' (OSB) construct and defined it as extra-role behaviour that is voluntary and contributes to organizational effectiveness but that might be rewarded by the organization. They have identified five forms of spontaneity: helping colleagues, defending the organization, making positive suggestions, developing one-self, and spreading goodwill. These behaviours are similar to those of OCB and POB. However, it is different from POB in that it excludes dysfunctional behaviours. It is also different from OCB. OCB includes volitional and spontaneous behaviour, whereas OSB incorporates behaviours that are not necessarily spontaneous. This fact has lead researchers to criticize this construct (Podaskoff et al. 2000).

Another construct which is similar to OCB is the Extra-Role Behaviour (ERB), which was first defined by Van Dyne et al. (1995). ERB is defined as behaviour that is intended to help organizations and exceeds existing role requirements (Organ et al. 2006). Despite the similarities, there are several important differences between OCB and ERB. For example, ERB includes two concepts that are not included in OCB, i.e., whistle blowing and principled organizational dissent. Whistle blowing involves informing the public or authorities about illegal activities inside the organization (Near & Miceli 1987). Conversely, principled organizational dissent is when employees raise their voice and protest the organization due to unfair practices (Graham 1986). The main purpose of these two concepts is to enhance the good of the organization and is not included in formal job description.

In summary, although different terms have been used to describe the tendency of individuals to engage in certain helping behaviours, each term differs from OCB in some ways. For instance, POB refers to both in-role and extra-role behaviours, including those which might not benefit the organization as long as the worker considers the behaviour as benefiting or helping others. Moreover, OSB and CP include behaviours that are formally rewarded by the organization, whereas OCB cannot be recognized by organization's reward system. Additionally, whistle blowing and principled organizational dissent, which are included in ERB, are not components of OCB.

Dimensions of Organizational Citizenship Behaviour

After its inception, the content of OCB has undergone through several changes. Additionally, there is an ongoing debate among scholars regarding the dimensions of OCB. In a pioneering study, in defining employee's innovativeness and spontaneity, Katz (1964) demonstrated five distinct dimensions, i.e., cooperating with others, protecting the organization, self-training, having favourable attitude toward the company, and volunteering constructive ideas. Smith et al. (1983) labelled Katz's conceptualization of employee's innovativeness and spontaneity as OCB. However, the first empirical study in this field identified altruism and generalized compliance as the two main dimensions of OCB (Bateman & Organ 1983; Smith et al. 1983). *Altruism* refers to helping behaviours directed towards specific individual within an organization (Organ 1988a; Smith et al. 1983). Examples of altruism are assisting a new coworker during socialization process and helping a colleague with explicit job task. *Generalized compliance* represents positive behaviour directed toward benefiting the whole organization, such as arriving at work on time, protecting company's property, and abiding by company's rules and regulations (Organ 1988a; Organ & Ryan 1995). A few years later, Organ (1988a) expanded the definition of OCB further and included three additional distinct dimensions to OCB: (i) *civic virtue* (individuals' behaviours that reflect their concerns and interests in the life of the organization, e.g., attending meeting, keeping up with organization's action, events, and changes); (ii) *courtesy* (employees' behaviour that is intended to avoid work–related problems with others, and/or being polite and considerate toward others); and (iii) *sportsmanship* (employee's readiness to endure the difficulties at the workplace without complaining).

The last couple of years have witnessed a shift in the dimensions of OCB. For example, Organ (1997) argued that OCB consist of three dimensions: helping behaviour, courtesy, and conscientiousness. Two years later, Organ and Pine (1999) contended the original two factor of OCB model is the most stable model (altruism and general compliance). Other OCB researchers have also put in a lot of effort to identify its dimensions. This has resulted in an increasing number of OCB dimensions, which made it difficult to identify the exact items that comprise the different dimensions of OCB (Podaskoff et al. 2000). On the other hand, Van Dyne et al. (1994) identified three factors underlying OCB i.e., obedience, loyalty, and participation. Conversely, Podaskoff et al. (2000) grouped approximately 30 diverse forms of behaviours into seven themes based on the types of behaviours: helping behaviour, sportsmanship, organizational loyalty, organizational compliance, individual initiative, civic virtue, and self-development. These dimensions are similar to the innovative and spontaneous behaviours identified by Katz (1964) and are vital for the survival of organization's social system (Rego & Gunha 2008). Along with Organ and Paine (1999), other studies also have reported two dimensions of OCB (Graham 1986; Smith et al. 1983; Van Scotter & Motowidlo 1996; Wiliams & Anderson 1991); some studies reported three dimensions (Organ & Konovsky 1989; Turnipseed & Murkison 1996), four dimensions (Mackenzie et al. 1991), and five dimensions of OCB (Borman & Motowidlo 1993; Organ 1988a). It is very clear that there are a lot of inconsistencies in the dimensionality of OCB among researchers. These inconsistencies in the measure of OCB support Podaskoff et al.'s (1993) observation that OCB's factors depend on the sample.

In their seminal work, Williams and Anderson (1991) proposed a two dimensional conceptualization of OCB which suggest that OCB could be viewed in terms of behaviours directed toward individuals (OCBI) versus those directed toward organizations (OCBO). Here it is essential to note that Williams and Anderson (1991) classified the dimensions of OCB based on Organ's (1988a) taxonomy and suggested that Organ's (1988a) taxonomy should be reduced to two dimensions, i.e., OCBI and OCBO. In addition, the majority of subsequent OCB research can be subsumed into these two categories (Podaskoff et al. 2009). For example, helping co-workers (George & Brief 1992), altruism and courtesy (organ 1988a), interpersonal helping (Graham 1989), interpersonal facilitation (Van Scotter & Motowidlo 1996), and social participation (Van Dyne et al. 1994) reflect OCB targeted at individuals (OCBI). In contrast, loyalty, obedience, participation (Van Dyne et al. 1994), job dedication (Van Scotter & Motowidlo 1996), conscientiousness, civic virtue, and sportsmanship (Organ 1988a), voice behaviour (Morrison & Phelps 1999), individual initiatives (Moorman & Blackely 1995), and promoting the company's image construct (Organ et al. 2006) indicate OCB targeted at organizations (OCBO). As a result, it is obvious that OCB consisted of two broader dimensions, OCBO and OCBI (Hoffman et al. 2007; Lee & Allen 2002; Podaskoff et al. 2009; Smith et al. 1983; Spitzmuller et al. 2008; Williams & Anderson 1991). The present study follows this conceptualization of OCB since these two dimensions capture the meaning of all other dimensions. Moreover, most literature follows this convention. The two dimensions are discussed in brief below.

a. Citizenship behaviours directed toward individuals (OCBI)

OCBI refers to a set of actions and activities that directly benefit a particular employee and ultimately contribute to organization's success (Lee & Allen

2002; Williams & Anderson 1991). Podsakoff et al. (2000) labelled this dimension as helping behaviour and defined it as willingly helping others with work-related problems. Other researchers have identified this category of behaviour in different ways. For example, Borman and Motowidlo (1993) named this dimension as helping and cooperating with others. Likewise, George and Brief (1992) termed this dimension as helping others, while Smith et al. (1983) referred to this dimension as altruism. On the other hand, Colquitt et al. (2009) defined this dimension as interpersonal citizenship behaviour.

b. Citizenship behaviours directed toward organization (OCBO)

The second dimension of OCB includes behaviours that benefit the organization as a whole (Lee & Allen 2002; Williams & Anderson 1991). Podsakoff et al. (2000) named this behaviour organizational compliance and it involves following company's rules and policies as well as defending the organization from external threats. Williams and Anderson (1991) were the first to coin this broad dimension as OCBO. These behaviours may include giving early notice when an employee needs to take a leave from work or informally adhering to organizations' rules and regulations. Similarly, Colquitt et al. (2009) referred to OCBO as behaviours that benefit organization by supporting and defending the organization, working to improve its operation and being loyal to it.

Regardless the number of dimensions, OCB is a multidimensional latent construct (Lee & Allen 2002; Motowidlo 2000; Organ et al. 2006; Williams & Anderson 1991). Moreover, researcher argued that when OCB is the main construct of a study, it is strongly recommended to stop thinking about the dimensions of OCB and focus on OCB only as a latent construct. However, the relationships that exist between OCB and its dimension are a controversial matter (Law et al. 1998). According to Edwards (2001) and Law et al. (1998) the dimensions of a construct can be conceptualize under an overall abstraction, and it is theoretically meaningful and parsimonious to use this overall abstraction as representation of the dimensions. An important condition for a multidimensional construct to be well-defined is to clarify the relationship between overall construct and its dimension (Johnson, Rosen & Chang 2011; Law et al. 1998). Specifically, it is necessary to determine whether the direction of causality starts at the construct and end at the dimensions (reflective model), or begins with dimensions and end at the construct (formative model) (Diamantopoulos & Siguaw 2006; Edwards 2001; Jarvis et al. 2003).

Overall, the theoretical relationship that exist between OCB as a multidimensional construct and its dimensions was not clearly identified by researchers like Organ (1988a, 1988b) and Williams and Anderson (1991); hence, it is possible to consider this relationship as reflective, in which OCB influences its dimensions, or formative in which the dimensions cause OCB (Law et al. 1998). On the other hand, in their seminal works, Hoffman et al. (2007) and LePine et al. (2002) suggested that OCB needs to be treated as a latent construct that underlies its two dimensions, OCBI and OCBO. This view was supported by other researchers (see Motowidlo 2000; Rego & Cunha 2010; Rego et al. 2009), and hence present study follows this convention.

In line with the above discussions and based on the definitions given by Williams and Anderson (1991), Lovell et al. (1999), Lee and Allen (2002), Krishnan and Arora (2008), LePine et al. (2002), and Hoffman et al. 2007, this book defines OCB as a multidimensional latent construct which is discretionary in nature and not recognized by a formal reward system. This behaviour is manifested in behaviours directed to benefit the organization as a whole (OCBO) and specific individual in the organization (OCBI).

ORGANIZATIONAL JUSTICE

In more recent years, organizational justice (OJ) has become an important phenomenon in the field of industrial and organizational psychology (Bolat 2010). Ince and Gul (2011: 109) defined it as "individual's perception about moral and ethical procedures". Typically, OJ refers to individuals' or groups' perception in relation to organization's fair and non-arbitrary practices in terms of allocation of organizational resources and procedures (Brockner et al. 1997; James 1993; Koys & DeCotiis 1991). Therefore, OJ is considered as a positive force that contributes toward organization's output (Eroglu 2009).

Related research in organizational science views the concept of justice as socially constructed (Colquitt et al. 2001), which suggests that any act is considered as being *just* only when the majority of individuals accepts it as it is (Cropanzano & Greenberg 1997). Greenberg (2001) suggested that an individual's perception of fairness and justice greatly depends on their norms and values. In this instance, individuals' perception of fairness is shaped by their experience and recurring exposure in relation to a particular standard which inculcate human's expectations related to a particular behaviour. Any act that conforms to this expectations is viewed as fair, whereas violation of these expectations is perceived as unjust (Beugre 2005; Greenberg 2001). In the case of organizations, OJ is mainly concerned with formulating rules and regulations in order to distribute resources, opportunities, and procedures (Folger & Cropanzano 1998).

Importance of Organizational Justice

Organizational survival, efficiency, effectiveness, and the quality of organizational life depend heavily on creating and maintaining a fair environment inside the organization (Mitrano 1997; Sheppard et al. 1992). In this regard it is crucial to instil and maintain justice in an organization; the absence of justice might pose a threat to the organization as well as to its employees (Sheppard et al. 1992). At the organizational level, violation of justice could increase organization's financial, economic, and social cost, while at the individual level it might affect employees' physical and psychological health negatively (Barclay & Skarlicki 2009; Sheppard et al. 1992). For example, research has shown that injustice at the workplace is associated with increased anxiety (Harlos & Pinder 2000), insomnia (Greenberg 2006), depression (Tepper 2001), and exhaustion (Elovainio et al. 2001). Therefore, OJ has received significant research interest in managerial literature.

Inculcating justice in an organization is very crucial for several reasons. (i) It helps build an organization's reputation among its employees' and acts as a symbol of authentication of that organization (Tyler & Lind 1992). (ii) It reduces employees' fear of exploitation and serves as an incentive for employees to cooperate with co-workers (Lind 2001a). (iii) It fulfills employees' various psychological needs, such as desire to control and need for appreciation, and it also satisfy individuals' interest to carry out moral and ethical responsibilities (Cropanzano et al. 2001; Folger & Cropanzano 1998; Lind & Tyler 1988;

Thibaut & Walker 1975). Additionally, nurturing justice inside organizations can lead to enhance employees' performance (Beugre 1998), encourages helping behaviour among employees (Greenberg 1990a), and assures an individual's sense of dignity and humanness (Shepard et al. 1992).

Moreover, empirical research found that OJ has a vital impact on employees' attitudes and behaviours at the workplace (Greenberg & Colquitt 2005). When people feel that they are being unfairly treated, their work commitment decreases, their job performances deteriorate, and they tend to be reluctant to cooperate with their fellow workers (Cropanzano & Greenberg 1997). Moreover, perception of injustice may affect employees' withdrawal behaviour (Colquitt et al. 2001), reduce employees' productivity (Fox, Spector & Miles 2001), and increase retaliatory behaviours (Aquino et al. 2005). On the other hand, when employees feel that they are being fairly treated by their organizations, they tend to show favourable attitudes toward the organization and this in turn increases their work efficiency and productivity (Greenberg 1990b). In addition, employees' perception of fair treatment stimulates their citizenship behaviour at work (Moorman 1991), increases trust among the members of the same organization (Folger & Cropanzano 1998; Tyler 1989), and helps resolve conflict (Folger & Konovsky 1989).

Conceptualization of Organizational Justice

Scholars are still debating the conceptualization of justice construct (Table 3). Greenberg (1987) introduced the OJ phenomenon as an indication for employees' perception of fairness. According to Colquitt et al. (2001), it facilitates the understanding of employees' work attitude, work behaviour, as well as their job performance. Typically, OJ refers to employees' perception of fairness at workplace, that is, whether they are being fairly treated by their organizations, and to what extent organizational events, procedures, interpersonal treatments, outcomes, and experiences are fair (Byrne & Cropanzano 2001; Folger & Geeenberg 1985; Folger & Cropanzano 1998; Moorman 1991). Beugre (1998: 13) gave a broader definition of OJ by stating that OJ is "the perceived fairness of the exchanges taking place in an organization, be they social or economic, and involving the individual in his or her relations with superiors, subordinates, peers, and the organization as a social system".

Table 3 Definitions of OJ in several selected past studies
(organized on the basis of year)

Author and year	Definition
Greenberg (1987)	Justice is "concerned with the ways in which employees determine if they have been treated fairly in their jobs and the ways in which those determinations influence other work related variables" (p.845).
Brockner et al. (1997); James (1993)	Employees' perception that organizational practices are equitable and non-arbitrary in terms of planning and distributing organization's resources and the procedures used to determine the distribution.
Folger & Cropanzano (1998)	OJ refers to individuals' perception of fairness at work, which includes fairness of outcomes, procedures, and interpersonal treatment.
Byrne & Cropanzano (2001)	Employees' perception of fairness at workplace and to what extent individuals consider events and experiences of the organization to be fair.
Greenberg & Colquitt (2005);	OJ is individuals' perception of fairness at the workplace.
Ince & Gul (2011)	OJ is individuals' perceptions regarding moral and ethical procedures.

Source: Compiled by the authors

Although past literature acknowledged justice as a three-dimensional concept (see Cohen-Charash & Spector 2001; Cropanzano et al. 2001; Masterson et al. 2000; McDowall & Fletcher 2004), there are also arguments for two-dimensional (Greenberg 1990a; Tyler & Bies 1990) and four-dimensional concept of this construct (Colquitt 2001; Colquitt et al. 2001) (Table 4). The three dimensions are distributive justice, procedural justice, and interactional justice. These dimensions are briefly discussed below.

Table 4 Dimensionality of OJ
in several selected past studies

Author and year	Dimensions
Ambrose & Schminke (2009); Ambrose & Arnaud (2005); Ambrose & Schminke (2006; 2007); Cropanzano & Ambrose (2001); Jones & Martens (2009); Kim & Leung (2007); Tornblom & Vermunt (1999)	One-dimension (overall organizational justice).
Greenberg (1990a); Tyler & Bies (1990)	Two dimensions: (i) distributive justice, and (ii) procedural justice.
Cohen-Charash & Spector (2001); Cropanzano et al. (2001); Masterson et al. (2000); McDowall & Fletcher (2004); Zhang, Nie & Yongtai (2009); Klendauer & Deller (2009)	Three dimensions: (i) distributive justice, (ii) procedural justice, and (iii) interactional justice.
Colquitt (2001); Colquitt et al. (2001)	Four dimensions: (i) distributive justice, (ii) procedural justice, (iii) informational justice, and (iv) interpersonal justice.

Source: Compiled by the authors

1. *Distributive justice* refers to employees' perception of organizational fairness in relation to allocation of resources and outcomes such as salary, goods/services, and promotion (Folger & Greenberg 1985; Folger & Cropanzano 1998; Greenberg 1990b). During its development, distributive justice was basically viewed from Adam's (1963, 1965) perspective of equity theory as ratio of outcomes to inputs. This theory postulated that equity is present when there is fair ratio between the inputs that employees bring into their organizations in terms of efforts, education, experiences, skills, etc., and the outcome that they receive from their organization in terms of salary, promotion, fringe benefit, etc., and comparing this ratio with same ratio of referent worker (Adam 1963, 1965).

2. *Procedural justice* refers to individuals' perception of fairness regarding procedures, methods, and policies that are used to determine outcomes

(Folger & Cropanzano 1998; Folger & Konovsky 1989). Thibaut and Walker (1975) argued that employees evaluate organizations' fairness not only based on the outcome that they received, but they also evaluate the procedures used to determine this outcome. Leventhal (1980) and Muchinsky (2000) suggested that any decision is perceived as procedurally fair if it is free from bias, contain correct information, and consistent over time and across people. Although the concepts of distributive justice and procedural justice are interrelated, they are two different and distinct constructs (Ambrose et al. 2007; Bies & Moag 1986; Folger & Konovsky 1989).

3. *Interactional justice* refers to the extent which individuals affected by the decisions made by organizations are treated with dignity, politeness, and respect (Bies & Moag 1986). In addition to the fairness of output and procedures used to determine this output, employees also consider interpersonal treatment received from their superior in evaluating the fairness of their organizations (Bies & Moag 1986). Greenberg (1993) suggested two components of interactional justice: interpersonal justice and informational justice. The former involves treating employees with respect, honour, and dignity during the enactment of procedures, and the later requires that employees are provided with sufficient and true information regarding the decision that might affect them.

Other schools of thought has recently questioned the merits of focusing on specific type of justice and encourage moving toward examining overall justice (Ambrose & Arnaud 2005; Ambrose & Schminke 2009; Cropanzano & Ambrose 2001; Hauenstein et al. 2001; Lind 2001a, 2001b). These researchers suggested that shifting the focus toward overall justice rather than a specific dimension might provide a clearer and better understanding of how employees experience justice in organizational setting. Furthermore, Ambrose and Schminke (2009) proposed different reasons for this shift toward overall OJ. First, literature related to OJ found that focusing on different types of justice might not reflect individuals' true experience of justice. Second, they proposed considering justice as an overall construct to overcome several existing limitations in examining this construct. Ambrose and Arnaud (2005) further elaborated these limitations. *Specifically,* this approach does not look at the relationship between the variable of justice theoretically or empirically. Theoretically, this approach considers each type of justice independently from the other types. Empirically, as this approach focus on the unique variance explained by each type of justice; it ignores the shared variance when explaining the result. Third, overall OJ considered the proximal driver of dependent variables, whereas certain types of justice play a distal role. Specifically, overall OJ may provide a better explanation of the relationship with other organizational phenomena such as satisfaction, commitment, and OCB rather than a specific type of justice (Ambrose & Schminke 2009).

Other researchers also have emphasized the essence of focusing on overall fairness. For example, Lind (2001a) found that individuals have different forms of justice experience at the workplace, such as distributive, procedural, and interactional justice. According to him, they combine these experiences to produce an overall sense of fairness that guide their behaviour inside the organization. In the same manner, Greenberg (2001) demonstrated that when employees form a feeling of justice, they are making holistic judgment based on whatever information that is available to them. Similarly, Shapiro (2001) said that individuals who suffer from injustice at the workplace are less likely to think about whether there are two or five or ten types of justice; they are more likely to react to their general experience of injustice. Additionally, Hauenstein et al. (2001) emphasized that focusing on overall justice is more valid than focusing on different types of justice. Furthermore, Ambrose and Arnaud (2005) and Ambrose and Schminke (2009) stressed the importance of considering overall justice to capture general individuals' justice experience and reaction. In following this convention and to overcome the limitations discussed regarding multi-dimensional justice construct, the present book considers justice as a uni-dimensional construct.

As stated early, researchers indicated the shortcomings associated with focusing on a specific type of justice and stressed the necessity to give more attention to a holistic approach to justice. Besides, the construct of overall fairness provides a more parsimonious approach toward understanding and the study individual's justice experience (Ambrose & Schminke 2006; Kim & Leung 2007). Furthermore, Colquitt and Shaw (2005) contended that scholars are more likely to show more flexibility when considering overall organizational fairness because variance can be explained without multicollinearity. Therefore scholars have suggested a global approach to conceptualize and measure justice (Ambrose & Schminke 2009; Ambrose & Arnaud 2005; Colquitt & Shaw 2005).

Islamic Banking Industry in Malaysia

Although Malaysia is a multi-ethnic country, Islam is the major religion in this country with approximately 61.4% followers (about 17 million people) (The pew forum on religion and public life 2010). Not surprisingly, Islam is declared as the "religion of the federation" (Wikipedia 2011). Malaysia is the second biggest hub of Islamic banking and finance (Khan & Bhatti 2008) and the Malaysian model of Islamic Banking is one of the most advanced Islamic banking systems in the world (Marimuthu, Jing, Gie, Mun & Ping 2010). Moreover, Malaysia has made significant contribution in the development of Islamic banking and finance around the world in terms of its rules and regulations (Khan & Bhatti 2008). The assets of Islamic banks had reached RM117, 393 million, which represents 11.8% of total assets in the Malaysian banking sector with its growth rate reaching 27% in last ten years (Khan & Bhatti 2008). These developments in Islamic bank's assets continue to grow and reached $65.6 in billion by 2012 with an average annual growth rate of 18-20% (Bank Negara Malaysia 2012). Due to the growth and economic contribution of this industry, it is important to understand, identify, and examine the variables that contribute to its success. Taking this into account, this study considers the Islamic banking industry as a research context which can be ascribed for two main reasons.

First, Islamic banking is characterized by ethical and social commitment (Ahmad 2000; Warde 2000) which strictly adheres to the Islamic *Shariah* principles (Marimuthu et al. 2010). Islamic economics scholars (e.g., Abdul Gafoor 2003; Aggarwal & Yousef 2000; Dar & Presley 1999; Zaher & Hassan 2001) suggested that the role of Islamic banking in the financial industry represents the most advanced, practical, and acceptable form of ethical banks rules. Therefore, this sector may have the potential to study the *IWE* phenomenon critically and widely. Additionally, *Islamic* banks are expected to adhere to the rules and regulation of *Islamic Shariah*, and to employ the available financial resources to benefit the Muslim society (Sudin Haron 1999). Consequently, Islamic banking has eliminated the roles of *riba*, (interest), *maisir* (gambling) and *gharar* (uncertainty) which are applied by the conventional banking system (Zakari bin Bahari 2009). On the other hand, Islamic banks emphasize and encourage *halal* deeds, and activities that are congruent with the *Shariah* such as profit loss sharing (PLS) and ethical contract (Mohd. Bakir Mansor 2008). Moreover, Islamic banks strictly prohibit financing any commodities, service, and/or individuals whose ethical practice are doubtful, such as the funding of the drugs, tobacco, casino industry (Kahf 1999). Therefore, it is worthwhile to consider the Islamic banking sector as a research context.

Second, the contribution of Islamic finance sector to the Malaysian's GDP has increased significantly to reach 2.1% share compared to 0.3% in 2000 (Bank Negara Malaysia 2012). Besides, Islamic banking system in Malaysia currently accounts for 20 percent of the overall banking system, which was the result of the Malaysian government's financial plan for the country (Bank Negara Malaysia 2012). Moreover, due to the significant contribution it has been making to the country's economic development, the number of Islamic financial institutions has been increasing steadily. As such, Malaysia presently has a good number of Islamic banking organizations, including full-fledged Islamic banks, Islamic banking windows, and Islamic banking subsidiaries (Zakari bin Bahari 2009). In 2000, there were two full-fledged Islamic banks and 17 commercial banks offering Islamic window (Zakari bin Bahari 2009). Currently there are 17 Islamic banks in Malaysia (Table 5). The development of Islamic banks began three decades ago, and this growth and development still continues; this has an enormous impact on country's development in terms of decreasing unemployment rate, lowering inflation rate, and making significant contribution to economic growth (Bank Negara Malaysia 2012).

An Overview of Malaysian Banking Industry

To achieve vision 2020, the Malaysian government has given emphasis to its banking sector. According to Vaithilingam, Nair and Samudra (2006) and Siddiqui (2001), the banking sector is an integral part of the economy and plays a key role in a nation's socio-economic development. They added that a fragile banking sector would have serious effects on a country's economy in the long run and has the potential to create a financial crisis that could cause the economy to collapse.

In Malaysia there are two banking systems operating side by side, the Islamic banking system and the conventional bank (Sudin Haron & Wan Nursofiza Wan Azmi 2008). The advantage of this system is that it provides more financial alternatives to the public; customers also have more options in choosing the bank that they would like to engage with. At the end of 2011, the Malaysian banking system consists of 25 commercial banks, 17 Islamic banks, 5 international Islamic banks, and 15 investment banks (Bank Negara Malaysia 2012).

Development of Islamic Banking Industry

The Islamic banking industry has become one of the fastest growing industries in Malaysia since the last three decades (Asyraf Wajdi Dusuki & Nurdianawati Irwani Abdullah 2007). Due to the benefits offered by Islamic banks, it has received considerable attention from different categories of customers (Iqbal & Molyneux 2005). Islamic banks accomplish the same major functions as other conventional banks; the only exception is that they apply the *Shariah* (Islamic law) rules and principles to carry out their functions (Iqbal & Mirakhor 2007). Islamic banking has become an important part of the overall Malaysian financial system due to its contribution to the growth and development of the Malaysian economy (Asyraf Wajdi Dusuki & Nurdianawati Irwani Abdullah 2007).

The Islamic banking institution in Malaysia was inspired by local and international factors (Marimuthu et al. 2010). Local factors include the establishment of the Pilgrim Fund Board in 1963 and the support from various parties to institute Islamic bank. Concurrently, the success stories of the Islamic banking sectors in Middle Eastern countries such as Egypt, Bahrain, and Dubai are the international factors which motivated the Malaysian government to establish such banking industry in Malaysia (Marimuthu et al. 2010). In 1983, Bank Islam Malaysia Berhad (BIMB) became the first Islamic banking system established in Malaysia (Khan & Bhatti 2008). Ten years later, the Malaysian government introduced the dual banking system which allows existing conventional banks to offer Islamic banking products to their customers (Khan & Bhatti 2008). Currently, there are seventeen Islamic banking institutions in Malaysia, six of them are entirely foreign-owned and two are international institutions (Bank Negara 2012). These banks offer more than 100 Islamic financial products and services which follow the Islamic guidelines and discipline (Marimuthu et al. 2010). These products and services are divided into five categories i.e., deposit, investment, financing, trade finance and card services (Marimuthu et al. 2010). Table 5 gives the list of Islamic banks in Malaysia as of 2012.

Table 5 List of Islamic banks in Malaysia

No	Name	Ownership
1	Affin Islamic Bank Berhad	Local
2	Al Rajhi Banking & Investment Corporation (Malaysia) Berhad	Foreign
3	Alliance Islamic Bank Berhad	Local
4	AmIslamic Bank Berhad	Local
5	Asian Finance Bank Berhad	Foreign
6	Bank Islam Malaysia Berhad	Local
7	Bank Muamalat Malaysia Berhad	Local
8	CIMB Islamic Bank Berhad	Local
9	Hong Leong Islamic Bank Berhad	Local
10	HSBC Amanah Malaysia Berhad	Foreign
11	Kuwait Finance House (Malaysia) Berhad	Foreign
12	Maybank Islamic Berhad	Local
13	OCBC Al-Amin Bank Berhad	Foreign
14	Public Islamic Bank Berhad	Local
15	RHB Islamic Bank Berhad	Local
16	Standard Chartered Saadiq Berhad	Foreign
17	Bank Muamalat Indonesia	Foreign

Source: Bank Negara Malaysia (2012)

Definition, Objectives and Principles of Islamic Banking

Islamic banking is a contemporary notion which was advanced three decades ago based on the rules and regulation of Islamic *Shariah;* its main principle is risk-sharing and it is not involved in funding based on a fixed, pre-determined return (Schaik 2001). This banking system aims to (i) make an ethical and impartial distribution of resources and achieve social fairness, (ii) promote Islamic ethic among staffs, client and the general public; (iii) alleviate poverty; (iv) contribute to social welfare; (v) improve the quality of products and services; (vi) help maximize profits in accordance with the *Shariah* principles; and (v) minimize costs of operations (Asyraf Wajdi Dusuki 2008; Iqbal 1997).

The Islamic principles and rules which govern the operations of Islamic banks are derived from various sources, i.e., the Holy *Quran, Hadith, Sunna, Ijma, Qiyas and Ijtihad* (Gait & Worthington 2007). All these sources emphasize on following the principles of *Shariah* which comprise of five basic activities. *First,* all transactions must be interest-free, i.e., free from *riba* (Marimuthu et al. 2010). *Second,* it must shun all activities that involve speculation or gambling (*gharar*) (Metwally 2006). *Third,* Islamic tax (*Zakat*) must be implemented (Samad 2004). *Fourth,* abide by the principle of profit and loss sharing (PLS) (Marimuthu et al. 2010). *Fifth,* the production or consumption of goods and services which are *haram,* such as financing of casino, night club or any other prohibited activity, must be avoided entirely (Samad 2004).

Differences between Islamic and Conventional Banking

Although Islamic banks perform the same functions as conventional banks, their approach is apparently different (Ahmad 2000; Henry & Wilson 2004; Iqbal & Molyneux 2005). The main difference is that Islamic banking follows the *Shariah* philosophy while conventional banking operates based on the laws and regulations set by the Bank Negara Malaysia (Zaharuddin Hj Abd Rahman 2007). Additionally, interest (*riba*), which is the basis of conventional banks, is strictly prohibited in Islamic banking (Samad 2004). Another important difference is that, while Islamic bank considers the relationship with customers as one between investor and entrepreneur, conventional bank perceives this relationship as that between borrower and debtor (Khir et al. 2008). Islamic banks typically provide funding based on the profit and loss sharing rules (PLS), which means that both parties have agreed to the share profit and loss which result from the investment made based on a pre-agreed ratio. On the other hand, conventional banks will provide financing based on interest (Khir et al. 2008). Last, but equally important, each Islamic bank is required to have a *Shariah Supervisory Board* to ensure that all business activities are in line with *Shariah* requirements, whereas conventional banks do not have to fulfill this requirement (Khir et al. 2008).

Shariah Concepts in Islamic Banking

The Islamic principles which govern the operations of Islamic banks are known as Shariah principles. According to Sudin Haron et al. (1994), the applicable principles include: (a) mudharabah or profit sharing, (b) musyarakah or joint venture, (c) murabahah or cost plus financing; (d) bai' bithaman ajil or deferred payment sale; (e) wadiah or safekeeping; (f) al-wakalah; (g) ijarah or leasing); and (h) qardhul hassan or benevolent. Table 6 demonstates the Islamic principles and their defintions, and the Appendix reveal all the definitions of the Islamic Termenologies used in this book.

Table 6 Shariah principles that guide activities of Islamic banks

Shariah principles	Defintion
Al-wakalah	An agreement between a principal (bank) and agent (customer) based on contract, in which the later authorized the former to operate their business on behalf of them (Sudin Haron et al. 1994).
Bai' al-Dayn	A transaction that involves the sale and purchases of Islamic securities, debt certificates, and various products that conform with Shariah. (IOSCO Islamic Capital Market Task Force 2012).
Bai' al-'Inah	A contract, which involves the sale and buy back transaction of assets by a seller. A seller will sell the asset to a buyer on a cash basis. The seller will later buy back the same asset on a deferred payment basis where the price is higher than the cash price. (IOSCO Islamic Capital Market Task Force 2012).

Bai' Bithaman Ajil	Represent the sale and purchase of merchandises on the basis of deferred payment at a price, which includes a profit margin agreed to by both parties (Sudin Haron et al. 1994).
Ijarah	Refers to an agreement between bank and customer. Based on this agreement the bank leases or rent an equipment, building or other facility to a customer for a fixed period and price, as agreed by both parties (Sudin Haron et al. 1994).
Mudharabah	Refers to a settlement between a provider of capital (bank) and an entrepreneur (customer), in which the principals provide 100% of the capital and the customer invest his experience and knowledge to operate the capital in investment project. This agreement is based on a profit-sharing according to a predetermined ratio (Sudin Haron et al. 1994).
Murabahah	Refers to specific type of sale of gooda at price, which consist of a profit margin based on agreement to by both parties (seller and buyer). Such sales contract is legal on the condition that the price, costs and the profit margin of the seller are specified in advance at the time of the agreement of sale (Sudin Haron et al. 1994).
Musyarakah	is a joint venture between two or more parties and the profit is shared according to the agreed ratio (Sudin Haron et al. 1994).
Qardhul Hassan	Refers to a loan which is free from interest. More clearly the debtor is required to pay back only the borrowed amount without bearing any extra cost (Sudin Haron et al. 1994).
Rahn	An act whereby a valued asset is used as warranty for a debt. The warranty will be employed to resolve the debt when a debtor is not able to pay back his debit (IOSCO Islamic Capital Market Task Force 2012).
Wadiah	Refers to situation in which bank is considered as a guardianof funds (*wadiah*). A person deposits funds in the bank and the bank guarantees refund of the whole amount of the deposit, when the depositor demands it (Sudin Haron et al.

Source: Compiled by the authors

The Products and Services of Islamic Banks

Generally, the product of Islamic banking was shaped by using the norms of muamalat such as al-wakalah, mudharabah, murabahah musyarakat, al-kafalah and other principles (Zakari 2009). In the case of Islamic banks in Malaysia, there are presently more than 50 products and services (Zakari 2009). These products include five categories that are offered by Islamic banks which include financing, investment, deposit and trade finance and card services (Sudin & Wan Nursofiza 2008). It is important to note that, different financial products apply different types of Islamic contracts. According to Saiful Azhar (2005) and Mohd Bakir (2008), the practical muamalat principles that are followed by the Islamic banks in Malaysia are as follow: (i) saving account applied wadiah yad dhamamah (WYD) and mudharabah; (ii) current account applied WYD; (iii) investment account applied mudharabah and wakalah; (iv) asset and vehicle financing applied bai bithamin ajil (BBA) and al-ijarah thumma al-bai (AITAB); (v) Islamic credit cards, personal and education financing applied bai al-innah and tawaruq; (vi) pawn broking applied rahnu; (vii) negotiable Islamic certificate of paper applied bai al-innah and bay al-dayn and, (viii) Islamic acceptance bill applied bai al-innah.

Islamic Work Ethic as the Driver of Workplace Attitude and Behavior

It is important for organizations to examine the impact of IWE on employee's attitude and behaviour at the workplace due to several reasons. *First*, countries such as Malaysia, Egypt, and Indonesia are moving in the direction of greater Islamization which requires more research to be done regarding Islamic values and principles (Saeed et al. 2001). *Second*, the Muslim population is spread all over the world and this makes it crucial to study and understand the ethic and values that determine the way they work and conduct business (Saeed et al. 2001). *Finally*, the wave of globalization has emphasized the importance of considering diversity at the workplace, including one based on religion (Uddin 2003). As such, it is important to understand the effect of IWE on individual's attitude and behaviour at the workplace.

Unfortunately, most research regarding work ethic was done from the perspective of PWE (Kumar & Rose 2009; Yunus et al. 2011). For instance, previous studies revealed a significant relationship between work ethic and OCB (see Furnham 1987; Moorman & Blakely 1995; Smith et al. 1983), as well as between work ethic and OJ (see Huseman et al. 1987; Schminke et al. 1997). Nonetheless, in these cases, work ethic was viewed from the perspective of Protestant work faith. Moreover, there is a paucity of research that addresses the relationships between IWE, OJ, and OCB. Therefore, it is necessary to examine work ethic from the Islamic perspective (Ali 2001; Kumar & Rose

2009). Hence, this study aims to fill this gap by verifying the relationships between OJ, OCB, and IWE.

As mentioned earlier, there is a dearth of research that study work ethic from the Islamic perspective, even in Islamic financial institutions. Financial institutions, in which the Islamic *Shariah* and principles are in practice, are considered a good choice to study IWE. Moreover, the Islamic financial sector contributes significantly to the Malaysian economic development, i.e., 2.1% of the country's GDP in 2009 (Bank Negara Malaysia 2012). Hence it is necessary to conduct more studies in this field to allow better management of employees based on Islamic rules and regulations.

Although past studies have found positive relationships between work ethic and OJ (Schminke et al. 1997) and OJ and OCB (Alotaibi 2001; Organ 1988a), there is a lack of research that have examined the mediating effect of OJ on the relationship between work ethic and OCB. Therefore, this study attempts to verify the mediating effect of OJ on IWE and OCB.

Altough Citizenship behavior and organizational justice are well studies in the the manufacture sector, it is yet to be conclusive in the service based literature. In the present study, building on theory and existing literature, two varibles are proposed as antecedents of citizenship behavior i.e. organizational justice and Islamic work ethic.

THEORETICAL UNDERPINNING

In this book, four relevant theories were chosen to address the consequnces of IWE and to support the proposed relationships. They are equity theory (Adams 1965), social exchange theory (Blau 1964), norms of reciprocity (Gouldner 1960), and other orientation theory (Meglino & Korsgaard 2004). These theories generated the idea to consider OJ and work ethic as the major antecedents of OCB. The next few paragraphs discuss these theories to explain how OJ and work ethic are linked to OCB.

Equity Theory

The main assumption of equity theory is that people want to be treated justly in their exchange with others (Penner et al. 1997). According to this theory, individuals engage in exchange relationships with the assumption that organizational outcomes should be fairly distributed based on their level of contribution (Adams 1965; Homans 1974; Walster et al. 1978). More specifically, employees consider their exchange relationship with their organization fair when their ratio of inputs to outcomes is similar to the ratio of inputs to outcomes of referent (referent is a person whom the employee considers as comparable in terms of his/her skills, experience, abilities, etc.) (Adams 1965). On the other hand, dissimilar ratios lead to perceptions of inequity which is presumed to create tension that motivates individuals to restore equity (Cowherd & Levine 1992). This restoration of equity could be achieved in different ways; for example, outcomes and contributions could be changed either objectively or psychologically. In fact, an individual might leave or withdraw psychologically from the situation (Greenberg & Colquitt 2005).

According to Organ (1988a, 1990), OCB could be considered as an input that employees could use to retrieve perceived injustice with their organization by increasing or decreasing their level of OCB to respond to the kind of treatment they receive from their employer. More clearly, employees will recompense their organization's fair treatment by performing OCB and will avenge a perceived injustice by withholding OCB (Organ 1988a). In this regard, justice is the predictor of OCB.

Social Exchange Theory and Norms of Reciprocity

Social exchange theories (Blau 1964) in conjunction with norm of reciprocity (Gouldner 1960) provide another theoretical framework that highlight why employees engage in OCB. It is important to note that, in understanding and justifying the social exchange relationships that take place in an organization, it is necessary to consider both theories simultaneously. Social relationships are distinct from other relationships that take place in an organization by exchange of intangible resources and are organized by rules of exchange such as norm of reciprocity (Blau 1964; Gouldner 1960). More specifically, social exchange relationship requires that one party (person, group, organization) provides a service for another party (person, group, organization) with the expectation of gaining future benefits of comparable value from them (Cho & Kessler 2008). Therefore, the norm of reciprocity is crucial to move the relationship forward. More clearly, the norm of reciprocity dictates that a person or organization who is the recipient of a benefit should reciprocate to diminish the feeling of obligation toward that individual or organization (Lester et al. 2008). In general, social exchange relationships evolve over time as two parties gradually become loyal to one another (Cropanzano & Mitchell 2005). If employees believe that they are being treated fairly, they develop a positive commitment to the organization (Organ 1988a) and increase their trust in their supervisor, which in turn increases the likelihood of OCB (Cardona et al. 2004).

Generally speaking, social exchange requires a trusting and stable relationship between partners which act as the foundation of the long term fairness in this exchange relationship (Konovsky & Pugh 1994; Pillai et al. 1999). According to Organ (1988a, 1990), social exchange motive influences employees to engage in OCB to reciprocate the perceived organizational fairness. Due to the norm of reciprocity, an individual who is treated fairly by his organization would feel obligated to respond with favourable attitude and behaviours (Konovsky & Pugh 1994; Moorman 1991; Moorman et al. 1998; Organ 1988a). Thus, in this regard, justice plays a crucial role in enhancing OCB.

Theory of Other Orientation

The theory of other orientation explains the degree to which individuals are concerned with the wellbeing of others (Meglino & Korsgaard 2004). This theory suggests that, in the pursuit of other oriented goals, individuals who possess high other orientation are less likely to think rationally and usually ignore the possible consequences to the self (Meglino & Korsgaard 2004). In other words, people high in other orientation are less likely to pursue self-interest in an organized way that requires evaluating personal costs and benefits when making choices (Meglino & Korsgaard 2006).

In this theory, individuals who are more other-oriented, either due to dispositional characteristics (individual differences) or due to the influence of contextual factors (such as group norms, OJ, etc.), are less likely to make rational assessment of the consequences of their activities (Sparrow et al. 2010). The theory of other orientation is derived from evolutionary theories of altruism that propose that individuals who are inclined to engage in self-sacrificing actions are less likely to process information in a reasonable fashion and are more likely to internalize, stick to, and enforce societal norms even if doing so is at their own expense (Fehr & Fischbacher 2003; Simon 1990, 1993).

It is worth noting that there are two basic forms of other orientation, i.e. *state* and *trait*. The state form is a function of contextual factors that drives individuals to be concerned about others. This form of drives includes OJ, group identity (Brewer 2004; Penner et al. 2005) and working on other-oriented tasks (Smeesters, Wheeler & Kay 2009). Employees who feel a high level of mental identification with their group/organization tend to follow the norms of that group/organization even if it meant sacrificing their personal choices (Terry et al. 1999). Conversely, the *trait* form focuses on predispositional variables such as empathy (Davis 1980), pro-social values (Meglino & Korsgaard 2004) and altruistic personality (Rushton 1984). Hence, it is evident that work ethic falls under both state and trait forms of other oriented values. In light of this, the present study assumes that work ethic can be considered as a potential variable that influences both OCB and OJ.

Organizational Justice and Organizational Citizenship Behaviour

More recently, researchers devote serious efforts to explore the contextual and dispositional variables as the potential predictors of extra role behaviour which eventually helps any organization to become more effective and efficient (Kumar et al. 2009; Podsakoff et al. 2000; Sharma et al. 2011). Among other contextual variables (e.g., job satisfaction, organizational commitment), OJ is found to be the stronger predictor of OCB (Organ 1988a; Organ & Ryan 1995; Podaskoff et al. 2000).

According to Greenberg (1990a), OJ is considered as an essential condition for the effective functioning of the organization as well as for its employees' satisfaction. Lambert et al. (2005) have agreed with this contention and stated that when justice is absent, organization will find it difficult to guide and motivate their employees. In general, employees depend on their perception of fairness inside the organization to determine whether management is reliable, non-biased, and treat them with respect and consider them as legitimate followers of the organizations (Lambert et al. 2005). Moreover, employees at workplace are expected to have close association with those individuals who work on fair basis (Karriker & Williams 2009). Therefore, scholars emphasize the importance of studying justice or fairness, as they believe that positive fairness perceptions can enhance organizational outcomes such as organizational commitment, job satisfaction and OCB (Colquitt et al. 2001). Consequently, this may lead to promising results such as organizational efficiency, effectiveness, and quality of work life (Sheppard et al. 1992).

The relationship between OJ and OCB can be explained by social exchange theory (Blau 1964) and equity theory (Adams 1965). In detail, when employees feel that they are being treated fairly; they reciprocate by performing extra role behaviour (social exchange theory). Again, when employees discover discrepancy between their inputs and outcomes in relation to referent, they may alter their OCB in order to reduce their dissonance (equity theory). In this regard, OJ plays an important role in influencing OCB.

In a Meta analytic review, Organ and Ryan (1995) have found fairness as the best predictor of OCB compared to other attitudinal variables like job satisfaction and organizational commitment. Furthermore, Podaskoff et al. (2000) contend that, practical research has concentrated on four key groups of antecedents of OCB: individual characteristics, task characteristics, organizational characteristics, and leadership behaviour. They have added that among these antecedents, fairness seem to be more strongly related to OCB than other antecedents. This notion is supported by other scholars as well (e.g., LePine et al. 2002; Staufenbiel 2000). Moreover Organ (1988a, 1990) found that fairness perception is the strongest predictor of OCB.

Besides the theoretical justifications, and logical explanations, empirical supports for the positive correlation between OJ and OCB also exist (see Alotaibi 2001; Scholl et al. 1987; Tepper & Taylor 2003). Furthermore, some meta-analytic review of the literature on attitudinal and situational antecedents of OCB reveal that OJ is relatively stronger predictor of OCB among a number of relevant variables (Ilies et al. 2007; LePine et al. 2002; Organ & Rayan 1995; Organ et al. 2006; Podaskoff et al. 2000). In a nutshell, all of these studies provide the idea that OJ is an influential predictor of OCB.

It is important to note that, based on different study context; different organizational variables may hold different meaning and may exhibit differences in term of their relationships (Nik Mu'tasim Abdul Rahman 2001). For example, people from different country may not possess same set of values and beliefs, and may have different views, interpretation, and preference that vary based on situations (Adler 1989). This notion is supported by other research findings which suggest that employees from diverse countries like Taiwan, Hong Kong, China, Britain, and Germany are influenced by justice perception differently, due to differences in their values (see Farh et al. 1997; Fischer & Smith 2006; Lum, Kervin, Clark et al. 1998; Tyler et al. 2000). Likewise, Korsgaard et al. (2010) also stressed the importance of studying OCB in different context, since this behaviour is rooted in the culture of the country.

Morrison (1994) argued that the relationship between justice and OCB vary on the basis of individuals and research context. The direct relationship between justice and OCB are examined in factory settings (Kamdar et al. 2006), educational context (Arif Hassan & Kamariah Mohd Noor 2008; Mohammad et al. 2010), health service institution (Lavelle et al. 2009), and hotel service sector (Hemdi & Nasurdin 2008). However, there is a dearth of studies in examining this relationship in Islamic financial sector. Therefore, it is necessary to study this realtionship in this specifc service context that is guided by the Islamic principles.

Islamic Work Ethic and Organizational Citizenship Behaviour

As mentioned earlier, dispositional variables have received research attention in predicting OCB (Konovsky & Organ 1996; Moorman & Blakely 1995; Neuman & Kickul 1998). Example of such variables includes conscientiousness, agreeableness (Neuman & Kickul 1998), positive and/or negative affectivity (Konovsky & Organ 1996; Organ & Ryan 1995), and individualism/ collectivism (Mororman & Blakely 1995). However, in their study Organ and Ryan (1995) found that among different dispositional variables only conscientiousness correlated significantly with OCB. It is important to note that, the research on the role of individual differences variables is at an earlier stage of development (Kumar et al. 2009; LePine et al. 2002; Podsakoff et al. 2000). Moreover, in comparison to the attitudinal variables, dispositional variables are not extensively examined in past literature in relation to OCB (Kumar et al. 2009; Organ & Ryan 1995). This clearly indicates the necessity of considering other dispositional variables in OCB research to enhance the understanding of the field. Taken this opportunity into account, and guided by other orientation theory, present study has considered work ethic as a dispositional antecedent of OCB.

The relationship between IWE and OCB can be explained by Meglino and Korsgaard's (2004) other orientation theory. This theory suggests that individuals' dispositions in other orientation are correlated with less self-interested and rational processing for information. For example, a person higher in other orientation (i.e., who expresses greater concern for the welfare of others) is more likely to reciprocate even in the absence of expected future returns. In other words, person who is higher in other orientation will be less likely to think about possible consequences to the self when making choices (Meglino & Korsgaard 2004). Drawing from the other orientation and social exchange theories, this study posits that expected returns and the occurrence of norm of reciprocity largely depends on other-oriented values. Thus, in this research it is assumed that, the person higher in other values such as IWE (either dispositional or due to situational factor) is more likely to reciprocate even in the absence of expected future returns (other orientation theory), whereas, individual who is low in other orientation values is less likely to reciprocate in the absence of future benefit (social exchange theory).

Besides the theoretical justification, empirical support also exists. Moorman and Blakely (1995) have tested the relationship between OCB and collectivist values and found support for the relationship between the two variables. In a seminal work, Smith et al. (1983) found that individuals from small cities and rural areas scored significantly higher on OCB than those individuals from big cities. The researchers attributed this result to individuals' tendency from rural to embrace the PWE more than individuals from big cities. Schnake (1991) and Greenberg (1993) also found support for this notion. They contended that, workers may consider it as moral obligation to work hard and to avoid laziness and lateness, thus those worker may be more likely to engage in some form of citizenship behaviour even under difficult or unfair conditions. In another study, Furnham (1987) found positive relationship between the PWE and a group of personality traits similar to the OCB. In a later studies, Ryan (2002), Turnipseed (2002), and Baker, Hunt and Andrews (2006) found positive association between individual's Protestant work ethic and OCB. Moreover, Kutcher et al. (2010) concluded that, religious affiliation, practice, and beliefs are significantly correlated with workplace outcomes in term of satisfaction, commitment, and OCB.

The above discussion provides the understanding that although western views of work ethic and Protestant work ethic (advanced by Max Weber during 1958) have been examined as the predictor of OCB, there is a dearth of research that has addressed IWE in relation to OCB. Therefore, it is necessary to examine the work ethic from Islamic standpoint. Besides that, only handful of studies has been devoted to IWE and its impact on individuals and organizations factors. Hence, this research aims to verify the direct relationship between IWE and OCB in the context of Islamic financial institutions.

At the workplace, employees are expected to perform according to the values of their organization (Hunt & Vitell 1986). Hence, it is proposed that creating an advanced level of IWE inside the Islamic bank can significantly influence the behaviours of individuals within the organization. It is evident that, IWE related to one's behaviour at work includes his or her cooperation, dedication, effort, and creativity (Nik Mu'tasim, Nordin Muhamad & Abdullah Sanusi Othman 2006). Essentially, when individuals have a strong relationship with Almighty (SWT), they tend to follow the instruction of religion (Nik Mu'tasim et al. 2006). Therefore, it is likely to say that those who believe in Islam and practice it are likely to exert more effort that exceed their work role to help colleagues, supervisor and their organization to prosper and develop.

Islamic Work Ethic and Organizational Justice

Islam emphasizes the importance of implementing and practicing justice in every aspect of life as the right way to achieve fairness and welfare for the society (Junaidah Hashim 2008). For example, the holy Quran continuously encourages people to be honest and fair in their trade and orders for fair distribution of wealth in society (Junaidah Hashim 2008). According to the holy Quran (4: 135), justice is indeed indispensable factor in Islamic teaching and should be implemented in daily life: "O ye who believe! Stand out firmly for justice, as witnesses to Allah, even as against yourselves or your parents, or your kin and whether it be (against) rich or poor". Moreover, justice plays a crucial role at the organizational level due to its ability to explain the behavioural outcomes such as commitment, OCB, job satisfaction, and employee performance (Colquitt, Noe & Jackson 2002).

The theory of other orientation (Meglino & Korsgaard 2004) can be used to justify the relationship between IWE and OJ. Built on this theory, individuals who are considered as high on other orientation are more likely to be influenced by social influences rather than rational thinking process that involve calculating cost and profit (Meglino & Korsgaard 2004). For instance, employees who are regarded as high on other oriented values are more concerned for the prosperity of other and less interested in maximizing outcome when deciding on courses of action (Meglino & Korsgaard 2004). Based on this theory, individuals higher in other oriented values like IWE (either dispositionally or as a result of contextual factors) are more likely to perceive their organization as fair even under difficult and/or unfair conditions. This argument is supported by other researchers (see Colquitt et al. 2006; Jawahar & Carr 2007; Orvis et al. 2008) who contend that individuals higher on prosocial traits are likely to be less affected by the level of fairness or benefits they obtain from their organization. On the other hand, individuals who possess self-interested traits are more affected by the quality of exchange with their organization (Eisenberger, Huntington, Hutchison & Sowa 1986; Kickul & Lester 2001; Raja et al. 2004). This situation can be better understood by using one analogy. For example, two employees (e.g., X and Y) are working in the same organization and in the same level of hierarchy. However, Y's salary is higher compare to X. Assuming X is high on prosocial trait and Y possesses self-interested trait, X may justify this situation by considering that, perhaps Y is more experienced / efficient than him and therefore, Y's salary is comparatively higher.

Besides the theoretical justification, empirical studies that support the relationship between work ethic and OJ also exist. According to Huseman et al. (1987), individuals vary in their sensitivity to equity which can be due to individuals' differences in term of their values, beliefs, and their orientation. Additionally, Joy and Wit (1992) examined how individual differences influence individuals' perception of procedural justice. Furthermore, Rasinski (1987) found positive relationship between individual's preferences for personality or for egalitarianism and how they weight procedural and distributive justice in judging the fairness of the government' polices. In support of this view, Schminke et al. (1997) also found positive relationship between individuals' ethical behaviour and their perception of organization justice.

On the basis of above discussion it can be said that, theoretical and empirical evidence suggests that individuals higher in other orientation are more likely to be less influenced by expectations of reciprocity. Besides that, most of the research that has evaluated this relationship has focused predominantly on the western concepts like PWE and formalist and/or utilitarian's view of ethic. Therefore, it is important to examine the work ethic phenomenon with the focus of Islamic standpoint (IWE) (Ali 2001). It is believed that individuals interpret and react to situations in different ways based on their ethical framework. For example, individuals high in IWE are believed to perceive their organization more fair compare to those who are low in IWE. Thus, it is being assumed that individuals, who view their organization implementing and following the Islamic precepts to conform ethical standard, would have positive effect on their perception of organization justice.

Organizational Justice, Organizational Citizenship Behaviour, and Islamic Work Ethic

Organ and Konovsky (1998) argued that the fair treatment can motivate subordinates inside the organization and make them obligate to reciprocate the organizational fairness through various positive behaviours, whereas, unfair treatment makes them unhappy and react in such a way that may harm the organizational performance. As suggested by Organ and Konovsky (1998), feeling of fair treatment stimulates OCB. A major stream of OCB research consistently found positive relationship between OJ and OCB (e.g., Greenberg 1993; Hemdi & Nasurdin 2008; Konovsky & Folger 1991; Niehoff & Moorman 1993; Organ & Konovsky 1989). Nonetheless, using the data from both longitudinal and cross sectional study in U.S., Tansky (1993) showed that overall fairness does not exert direct influence on OCB. In a similar manner, in the context of insurance service in U.S., Schappe (1998) contended that there is no relationship between procedural justice and OCB. Similarly, Moorman (1999) and Niehoff and Moorman (1993) also did not find significant relationship between distributive justice and OCB. Moreover, in a Malaysian study, Arif Hassan and Kamariah Mohd Noor (2008) have examined the relationship between justice and extra-role behaviour among lower and middle managers from six organizations. However, they did not find significant relationship between these two constructs. In a similar vein, Mohammad et al. (2010) failed to find significant relationship between distributive justice and OCB in the higher educational sector. Therefore, to resolve the conflict of past study findings, it is necessary to consider the effect of a third variable as a moderator that can strengthen this relationship.

Although the influence of OJ on employees' behaviour at workplace is well established, it remains unclear why some individuals respond to same treatment in different way (Colquitt & Greenberg 2003). Moreover, Scott and Colquitt (2007) raised question about why some people respond to injustice by involving in unethical behaviour, some other employees decrease their level of voluntary behaviour, whereas, other type of employees do not react negatively to response to injustice and continue to perform extra-role behaviour that can benefit the organization. In response to this question, Scott and Colquitt (2007) suggested to include a potential moderator variable of justice effect. In such situation, Organ (1990) suggested that dispositional variables may play vital role as a moderator on the link between work context variables and OCB. Therefore, following Organ's (1990) suggestion this study proposes to consider a dispositional variable (i.e., IWE) as a moderator in this link.

IWE is a dispositional variable that may moderate the relationship between OJ and OCB. IWE organizes and directs employees' attitudes and behaviours at workplace based on holy *Quran* and *Sunnah* (Abuznaid 2009). The main focus of IWE is to emphasize on hard work, work commitment, cooperation and innovative work (Yousef 2001). In doing so, IWE can influence the ethical behaviours of Muslim workers inside the organization in positive ways (Abuznaid 2009).

The moderating effect of IWE can be justified theoretically by using other orientation theory, which refers to one's tendency to be concerned with welfare of others (Meglino & Korsgaard 2004). According to Miller (1999), most theories related to behaviours in the social and organizational sciences assume that individuals will behave consistently with their rational self-interest. This means that a person will act in such a manner that is expected to lead to an optimal result for the individual (Bazerman 1993). On the other hand, individuals who are lower in rational self-interest is likely to sacrifice their own interests by developing other oriented values characterized by sympathy and concern for the welfare of others (Meglino & Korsgaard 2004). Built on this theory, it is argued that employees who are higher on other values such as IWE would be less affected by unfair treatment compare to individuals who are low in IWE. Moreover, individuals who are higher in other oriented values such as IWE have the tendency to perform OCB regardless of whether they get anything from their organization in exchange or not. The positive work orientation is grounded in individuals' values and ethical aspects.

Based on these discussions, it is expected that incorporating IWE as a moderator in the relationship between OJ and OCB will strengthen this relationship positively which may contribute in solving the discrepancies in the existing literature.

Organizational Justice, Islamic Work Ethic, and Organizational Citizenship Behaviour

It is evident that individual's ethical behaviour may affect employees' perception of OJ in a positive way (Schminke et al. 1997). Moreover, in regard to IWE, it is expected that when the individuals possess high IWE they tend to abide by the organizational rules and regulations, and they are more likely to perceive their organization as ethical, and they are probably less affected by the quality of fairness or benefit they receive from their organization compared to other employees who are considered low in IWE. Additionally, other researchers (e.g., Cropanzano et al. 2002; Masterson et al. 2000) found positive link between OJ and quality of employees' social exchange relationship toward their organization. In this regard, the resulting social relationship has been found to be a good predictor of employees' attitudes and behaviours such as commitment, satisfaction and OCB (Tekleab et al. 2005). Thus it is likely to say that OJ can mediate the relationship between IWE and OCB.

Other orientation theory and social exchange theory generate the idea to consider OJ as a mediator between IWE and OCB. On the basis of social exchange theory, the relationship between employees and their organization exceeds the formal employment contract, in which employees' contribution and obligation are not clearly mentioned (Blau 1964). Conversely, other orientation theory distinguishes between rational and self-interested judgment and other oriented processing (Korsgaard et al. 2010). According to Meglino and Korsgaard (2006), rational self-interested behaviour defined as thinking and acting in a manner that is expected to lead to optimal result for individuals. Contrary to this, individuals who assign high priority to other oriented values pay less attention for personal cost and benefit (Meglino & Korsgaard 2004). According to the other orientation theory, employees who are higher on other oriented values such as IWE are more likely to be less affected by the level of fairness or outcome they receive from their organization. This contention is supported by previous research who argued that individuals higher in other oriented values tend to be less influenced by expectation of reciprocity and more sensitive to the obligation to reciprocate (see Colquitt et al 2006; Kamdar & Van Dyne 2007; Korsgaard et al. 2010). Besides, based on social exchange theory, when employees consider their organization fair to them, they tend to feel morally obliged to reciprocate the fair treatment by adopting behaviours that help that organization to progress and prosper, such as helping new colleague during the socialization process, protecting the organization property from damage, and uttering good words about their organization in front of others. As such, the theoretical evidence for the mediating role of OJ exists.

Inclusion of OJ as a mediator may be justified by the empirical evidences as well. For instances, the direct relationship between work values and OCB is supported (see Kirkman, Lowe & Gibson 2006; Merrens & Garrett 1975; Sparrow et al. 2010; Sparrow & Wu 1998; Varma, Pichler, Budhwar & Biswas 2009). Moreover, the direct relationship between work ethic and justice (see Baker et al. 2006; Schminke et al. 1997) as well as the direct relationship between OJ and OCB (see Fahr et al. 1990; Moorman 1999; Organ 1988a, 1988b, 1990; Rego & Cunha 2010) are supported.

How to Inculcate Ethics
and Citizenship Behaviour?
Suggestions for Islamic Banking Industry

The Islamic banking sector is a comparatively understudied area in regard to employees' ethical behaviour as well as their extra role behaviour. As such, this book may be considered as a pioneer one that highlights the relationship between IWE and OCB in the Islamic banking sector. It is expected that this book will provide managers important information regarding the role of IWE in order to instil and practice it for the benefit of their organization. For example, practitioners can organize training programs to reinforce employees' understanding of Islamic ethic at the workplace so that a high level of OCB will be attained. Furthermore, organizations can directly influence their employee's citizenship behaviours by understanding the antecedents of OCB which would eventually increase positive work behaviours among the workforce, and thus contribute to organizational effectiveness and employees' performance. Last but not least, Islamic financial institutions and other organizations that apply the Islamic *Shariah* and principles could benefit from the discussion of this book.

Firstly, it emphasizes the importance of considering both the situational and dispositional variables to enrich the level of citizenship behaviour within organizations. Organizational citizenship behaviour refers to employees' extra role behaviour, which could help organizations to excel in their environment (Mohammad et al. 2010). Organizations that rely only on their employees' in-role behaviour are likely to suffer in the long run, whereas organizations that encourage and motivate their employees to perform activities that exceed their main job duties are expected to excel, progress, and outperform other competitors in the market (Katz 1964; Mohammad et al. 2011). Therefore, managers should give due attention to individual and situational factors that could foster such favourable behaviour (i.e., OCB). More specifically, managers should create fair environment to enhance employees' perception of justice in their organization in addition to stressing the importance of inculcating the rules and principles of Islam in conducting their business.

The second implication is related to employees' perception of justice. Justice refers to the perceived fairness of an organization as a whole (Lind 2001a). This research found that employees who perceive their organization as being fair to them are more willing to display citizenship behaviours. On the other hand, employees who feel that their organizations are not being fair to them are more likely to withhold and/or reduce their contributions of citizenship behaviour. Therefore, managers should take serious steps to ensure that justice is prevalent throughout their organization. In general, employees can differentiate between the sources of justice (i.e., distributive, procedural, interactional), but what guide their behaviour inside the organization is a holistic judgment about the level of fairness of their organization based on the information available to them (Lind 2001b). There are several steps that managers could take to ensure that justice is fairly practiced in their organizations are:

(i) Managers need to give their subordinates the opportunity to express their opinion on matters and issues that are related to their careers. Individuals need to feel that they are valuable assets to their organizations, and that their ideas, thoughts, and opinions are appreciated. This motivates them to perceive their organization as being fair to them, and they are likely to reciprocate by showing positive attitudes and behaviours (see Thibaut & Walker 1975).

(ii) The authorities should give their employees the opportunity to take part in important decisions that affect them and the organization as a whole. When individuals are involved in a decision making process, they are more likely to put in more effort and be more committed in accomplishing organization's goals. They will be more inclined to be responsible and accountable of the outcome of their decision, and more prone to perceive their organization as being fair to them (see Greenberg & Folger 1983).

(iii) Organization's policies, procedures, and decisions are required to be consistent over time and across people, free of bias, ethical, correctable, and accurate. Managers are required to make ethical and moral decisions that have no harmful effects on internal or external customers, while at the same time being impartial and objective in their decisions; their decisions must be based on accurate information and can be modified when necessary. This environment is expected to enhance individual's general experience of justice (see Leventhal 1980).

(iv) Employees must be treated with respect and dignity and must be given sufficient information and explanation regarding decisions and their outcomes. Additionally, organizational outcome in term of salaries, promotion, bonus, vacations, etc. should be allocated fairly and based on clear rules and regulations that govern the whole organization. Hence, employees will be more inclined to view their organization as being fair to them (see Adams 1965; Bies & Moag 1986).

(v) The management could organize meetings, seminars, conferences, and ceremonies on a regular basis with their workforce to discuss organization's current situation and future plans to improve the functionality of the organization and move forward. This would eliminate physical and psychological barriers between managers and their subordinate, create a conducive environment to share and exchange information, and produce innovative ideas that could help employees and their organization as well as foster brotherhood among employees.

(vi) The authority could create a new department to receive and handle employees' complaints and grievances. Alternatively, organizations could create suggestion box through which employees could channel their suggestion, complaints, and grievances.

(vii) As organizations function in dynamic and constantly changing environment, they should revise and refine the systems and rules and regulations that govern work and business to improve and better prepare themselves in facing and dealing with the changes that take place in the local and global environment. For example, using obsolete technology to run business and/or using old compensation system is not considered as fair from employees' perspective.

(viii) Last but not least, the authority should always emphasize the role of Islamic values in enhancing fair workplace environment as well as generating ethical and moral individuals. Past studies (see Colquitt et al. 2001) found that individuals who are high on prosocial trait perceive their organization as fair even when the environment is uncertain. Indeed, Islamic banks operate in a dynamic and fluctuating environment. Therefore, they need people who are ethical and more resilient in facing uncertainty during difficult situations.

The third practical contribution is related to Islamic work ethic. The employees of Islamic banks have a high degree of Islamic work ethic which makes them more inclined to demonstrate organizational citizenship behaviour even when future benefits are unclear, and they are more prone to perceive their organizations as fair even when dealing with difficult situations. In other words, this study underlines the important role of individual difference variable (i.e., IWE) in affecting attitudinal and behavioural outcomes (i.e., OJ and OCB respectively). Therefore, it is essential that managers reinforce, instil, and foster the magnificent values of Islam in their organization. This could be done by:

(i) Adhering to the rules and instructions of *Shariah* in every aspect of their organizational life. In this regard the Islamic *Shariah* stresses on noble values such as considering work as worship; fairness and justice are important conditions for society welfare; humbleness and modesty reflect the civil level within organization; hard work and patience are important conditions for individuals to be rewarded and be pardoned by Allah SWT; continuous improvement and cooperation; forgiveness and coexisting in peace; generosity and flexibility; commitment and dedication; and performing all transaction based on the rules set by *Shariah* principles. On the other hand, Islamic work ethic prohibits and constrain all unethical behaviours that contradict the principles of Islamic *Shariah,* such as interest, gambling, stealing, lying, gossiping, vandalism, etc. (See Ali 1996, Yousef 2001).

(ii) Assessing and implementing training programs to enhance employees' understanding of Islamic ethic at the workplace in the effort to achieve a high level of OCB. Human beings face many changes in their lives; sometime they might deviate from the right path due to internal or external factors, and this could have negative effect on their productivity and performance in an organization. Therefore, the management should conduct training program on a regular basis not only for new staff, but also for senior staff in order to instil, reinforce, refresh, and remind them of Islamic values and the importance of these values in our live as well as to gain the pleasure of Allah (SWT) in this life and the in hereafter. Practicing the noble values of Islam not only strengthen an individual's relationship with Allah SWT, it also lead to peace and tranquillity in a person's life, which in turn affect their performance and effectiveness in an organization positively and profoundly.

(iii) Consolidate different functions such as talks, seminars, meetings, and distributing booklet, brochures, and internal publications that could enrich employees' knowledge regarding Islamic ethic at the workplace. The objective of these efforts is to enhance individuals' knowledge and provide them with up-to date information regarding Islamic values and the Islamic principles that govern the operation of Islamic banks such as *Mudharabah, musyarakah, murabaha.*

(iv) Human resource managers should consider hiring employees with strong Islamic work ethic when they hire staff for new positions that require more OCB. In general, Islamic work ethic is an individual difference variable that requires a long time to be developed. Hence, by recruiting individuals who already have strong Islamic work ethic, organizations could reduce the cost of training, boost organizational citizenship behaviour, and enhance employees' general experience of fairness.

(v)   Promoting and adopting Islamic work ethic not only increase employees' level of satisfaction, commitment, loyalty, and organizational citizenship behaviour, it could also reduce negative behaviour, such as counterproductive behaviour and withdrawal behaviour, that could hamper organization's productivity and profitability. Ultimately this has the potential to ameliorate the efficiency and effectiveness of organizations and improve their performance (see Aboznaid 2009)

The fourth practical contribution is related to the research context. To the best of the researcher's knowledge, this is the first study that tests the relationship between organizational justice, Islamic work ethic, and organizational citizenship behaviour in the Malaysian Islamic banking sector, which has the potential to contribute significantly to the country's development. The findings of this study are expected to be of great importance to all financial organizations such as Takaful Insurance and Tabung Haji that operate based on Islamic *Shariah*. Moreover, the findings of this research are expected to motivate other service and industrial organizations to operate based on the Islamic rules and instructions.

FURTHERING THE THOUGHTS OF FUTURE RESEARCH

Malaysia is considered as one of the pioneering countries to establish Islamic banking system which adopted the Islamic *Shariah* principles in their activities and transactions, this research focused only on Malaysia. In general, past studies demonstrate a paucity of theoretical and empirical studies regarding the effect of work ethic on organizational citizenship behaviour (see Sparrow et al. 2010)

Moreover, work ethic, organizational justice, and organizational citizenship behaviour are embedded in culture and may vary from one country to another (see Sparrow 2006; Sparrow et al. 2010). Therefore, future researchers are urged to replicate this research in different cultural context. For example, in China the values and beliefs that dominate the life of Chinese is *Buddhism*, whereas in India its *Hinduism*. While the values of *Hinduism* focus mainly on achieving materialistic benefits (Ashta 2010), *Buddhism*'s main concern is to achieve salvation by satisfying spiritual needs (Abd Rahman 2010). It is necessary to study the relationship among these constructs in countries such as China and India to enhance and enrich existing knowledge regarding these constructs.

References

Abbasi, A. S., Hameed, I. & Bibi, A. 2001. Team management: The Islamic paradigm. *African Journal of Business management* 5(5): 1975-1982.

Abdel Rahman Ahmad Abdel Rahman 1995. An Isalmic perspective on organizational motivation. *The American Journal of Islamic Social Sciences* 12(2): 185-203.

Abdul Gafoor, A. L. M. 2003. Meeting the financial needs of Muslims: A comprehensive scheme. *International Journal of Islamic Financial Services* 5(3): 29 – 36.

Abdul Shukor Bin Shamsudin, Abdul Wahid Bin Mohd Kassm & Nor Azmi Johari 2010. Preliminary insights on the effect of Islamic work ethic on relationship marketing and customer satisfaction. The *Journal of Human Resource and Adult Learning* 6(1): 106-114.

Abeng, T. 1997. Business ethics in Islamic context: Perspective of a Muslim business leader. *Business Ethics Quarterly* 7(3): 47-54.

Abu-Saad, I. 2003. The work values of Arabic teachers in Israel in multicultural context. *Journal of Beliefs and Values* 24(1): 39-51.

Abuznaid, S. A. 2009. Business ethics in Islam: The glaring gap in practice. *International Journal of Islamic and Middle Eastern Finance and Management* 2(4): 278-288.

Adams, J. S. 1963. Toward an understanding of inequity. *Journal of Abnormal and Social Psychology* 67: 422-436.

Adams, J. S. 1965. Inequity in social exchange. In L. Berkowittz (Ed.), *Advance in experimental psychology* (2: 267-299). San Diego, CA: Academic Press.

Adler, N. J. 1989. Cross-culture interaction: The international comparison fallacy? *Journal of International Business Studies* 20(3): 515-537.

Aggarwal, R. K. & Yousef, T. 2000. Islamic banks and investing financing. *Journal of Money, Credit and Banking* 32(2): 93 – 100.

Ahlul Bayt Digital Islamic Library Project 2012. http://www.al-islam.org/ghadir/reliability.asp?person=150 [8 April 2012].

Ahmad, K. 1976. *Islam: Its meaning and message.* London: Islamic Council of Europe.

Ahmad, K. 2000. Islamic finance and banking: the challenge of prospects. *Review of Islamic Economic* 9: 57-82.

Al-A'ali, M. 2008. Computer ethics for computer professionals from an Islamic point of view. *Journal of Information, Communication & Ethics in Society* 1: 28-45.

Albahi, S. & Ghazali, A. 1994. *Islamic values and managment.* Institute of Islamic Understanding, Kuala Lumpur.

Al-Buraey, M. A. 1990. *Management and administration in Islam.* King Fahd University of Petroleum and Minerals. Dhahran- Saudi Arabia.

Al-Ghazali Abu Hamid Muhammad ibn Muhammad, 1982. *Ihya Ulum al-Din.* Al-Qahirah: Dar al-Hadith.

Al-Jazairy, A. 1988. *This is the beloved prophet Muhammad (PBUH).* Damnhour, Egypt: Lynah Library for Publication and Distribution.

Ali, A. J. 1988. Scaling an Islamic work ethic. *Journal of Social Psychology* 128(5): 575-583.

Ali, A. J. 1992. Islamic work ethic in Arabia. *Journal of Psychology* 126(5): 507-520.

Ali, A. J. 1996. Organizational development in the Arab-world. *Journal of Management Development* 15(5): 4-22.

Ali, A. J. 2005. *Islamic Perspectives on Management and Organization.* Edward Elgar, Cheltenham.

Ali, A. J. & Al-Kazemi, A. 2007. Islamic work ethic in Kuwait. *Cross Cultural Management: An International Journal* 14(2): 93-104.

Ali, A. J. & Al-Owaihan, A. 2008. Islamic work ethic: A critical review. *Cross Cultural Management: An International Journal* 15(1): 5-19.

Ali, A.Y. 1987. *The Quran: Text, translation, and commentary.* Elmhurst, NY: Tahrike Tarsile Quran, Inc.

Ali, M. M. 1998. Mawdudi's philosophy of education: the dynamics change and leadership. *Muslim Education Quarterly* 15(4): 24-40.

Allen, T. D., Barnard, S., Rush, M. C. & Russell, J, E. A. 1999. Rating organizational citizenship behavior: Does the source make a difference? *Human Resource Management Review* 10(1): 97-114.

Al-Modaf, O. A. 2005. Islamic work ethic code: A conceptual study. Umm Al-Qura University *Journal of Education, Social Sciences and Humanities.* Special issue on the occasion of celebrating Makkah Al-Mukarramah as the capital of Islamic culture for the year 1426 H., corresponding to 2005.

Alotaibi, A. G. 2001. Antecedent of organizational citizenship behavior: A study of public personnel in Kuwait. *Public Personnel Management* 30(3): 363-376.

Ambrose, M. L. & Arnaud, A. 2005. Distributive and procedural justice: construct distinctiveness; construct interdependence, and oval justice. In Greenberg & J. Collquitt (Eds.) *The handbook of organizational justice* (PP. 59-84). Mahwah, NJ: Erlbaum.

Ambrose, M. L., Hess, L. & Ganesan, S. 2007. The Relationship between justice and attitudes: An examination of justice effects on event and system-related attitudes. *Organizational Behavior and Human Decision Processes* 103(1): 21-36.

Ambrose, M. L. & Shminke, M. 2006. The role of overall fairness judgments in organizational justice research.Paper presented at the 21ˢᵗ annual meeting of the society for industrial and organizational psychology, Dallas, TX.

Ambrose, M. L. & Schminke, M. 2007. Examining justice climate: Issues of fit, simplicity, and content. In F. Dansereau, & F. J. Yammarino (Eds.), *Research in Multilevel Issues.* New York, NY: Elsevier.

Ambrose, M. & Shminke, M. 2009. The role of overall justice judgment in organizational justice research: A test of mediation. *Journal of Applied Psychology* 94(2): 491-500.

Andrisani, P. 1978. *Work attitudes and labor market experience.* New York: Praeger Publications.

Andrisani, P. & Pames, H. 1983. Commitment to the work ethic and success in the labor market: A preview of research findings, in: J. Barbash, R. Lampman, S. Levitan & G. Tyler (Eds.) *The Work Ethic: a Critical Analysis*, PP. 154-161 (Madison, WI, IRRA).

Ang, S., Van Dyne, L. & Begley, T. M. 2003. The employment relationships of foreign workers versus local employees: A field study of organizational justice, job satisfaction, performance, and OCB. *Journal of Organizational Behaviour* 22: 561-583.

Aquino, K., Bies, R. & Tripp, T. 2006. Getting even or moving on? Power, procedural justice, and types of offense as predictors of revenge, forgiveness, reconciliation, and avoidance in organizations. *Journal of Applied Psychology* 91:653-668.

Arif Hassan & Kamariah Moh Noor, 2008. Organizational justice and extra-role behavior: Examination the relationship in the Malaysian cultural context. *IIMU Journal of Economics and Management* 16(2): 187-208.

Ary, D., Jacobs, L. C. & Razavieh, A. 1996.. *Introduction to research in education.* Orlando, Florida: Harcourt Brace College Publishers.

Ashta, A. 2011. Hinduism and Micrfinance. http://ssrn.com/abstract=1728384. [April 14 2012].

Askari, H. & Taghavi, R. 2005. The principle foundations of an Islamic economy. *Banca Nazionale del Lavoro Quarterly Review* 58(235): 187-206.

Assamalloty, N. 1998. *Structures and Systems of the Islamic Society.* Jeddah: Dar Al-Sharooq.

Asyraf Wajdi Dusuki 2008. Understanding the objectives of Islamic banking: A survey of stakeholders' perspectives. *International Journal of Islamic and Middle Eastern and Management* 1(2): 1-25.

Asyraf Wajdi Dusuki & Nurdianawati Irwani Abdullah 2007. Why do Malaysian customers patronise Islamic banks? *International Journal of Bank Marketing* 25(3) 142-160.

Atiyah, H. 1999. Public organization's effectiveness and its determinants in a developing country. *Cross Cultural Management* 6(2): 8-21.

Az-Zubaidi, Z. 1996. *Summarized Sahih Al-Bukhari.* Translated by Muhammad Khan. Riyadh: Saudi Arabia.

Bahagat, R. S. 1979. Black-White ethnic differences in identification with the work ethic: Some implications for organizational integration. *Academy of Management Review* 4:381-391.

Baker, T. L., Hunt, T. G. & Andrews, M. C. 2006. Promoting ethical behavior and organizational citizenship behaviors: The influence of corporate ethical values. *Journal of Business Research* 59: 849-857.

Bank Negara Malaysia. 2012. Islamic Banking & Takaful. http://www.bnm. gov.my/microsites/financial/0204_ib_takaful.htm [27 January 2012].

Bank Negara Malaysia 2012. Governor's Keynote Address at the World Congress of Accountants (WCOA): "Islamic Finance: Strengthening the Global Financial Market". http://www.bnm.gov.my/index. php?ch=9&pg=15&ac=387&print=1 [27 January 2012].

Bank Negara Malaysia. 2012. List of licensed banking institutions in Malaysia. http://www.bnm.gov.my/index.php?ch=13&cat=banking [27 January 2012].

Bank Negara Malaysia. 2012. List of licensed banking institutions in Malaysia. http://www.bnm.gov.my/index.php?ch=13&cat=banking&type=IB&fund=0&cu=0 [27 January 2012].

Bank Negara Malaysia. 2012. Islamic Banking & Takaful. http://www.bnm.gov.my/microsites/financial/0204_ib_takaful.htm#overview [27 January 2012].

Barclay L. & Skarlicki, D. P. 2009. Healing the wounds of organizational injustice: Examining the benefits of expressive writing. *Journal of Applied Psychology* 94: 511-523.

Barclay, L., Skarlicki, D. & Pugh, S. D. 2005. Exploring the role of emotions in injustice perceptions and retaliation. *Journal of Applied Psychology* 90: 629-643.

Bashir, A. 1998. Ethical norms and enforcement mechanism in profit-sharing arrangements. *The Mid-Atlantic Journal of Business* 4(3): 255-271.

Bateman, T. L. & Snell, S. A. 2002. *Management: Competing in new era.* (5th ed.). New York: Prentice Hall.

Bateman, T. S. & Organ, D. W. 1983. Job satisfaction and the good soldier: The relationship between affect and employee citizenship. *Academy of Management Journal* 26: 587-595.

Bazerman, M. H. 1993. Fairness, social comparison and irrationality. In J. K. Murnighan (Ed.), *Social psychology in organizations* (pp. 184-203). Englewood Cliffs, NJ: Prentice Hall.

Beekun, R. I. 1997. *Islamic business ethics.* IIIT, Herndon, Virgina, USA.

Beekun & Rafik Issa. 1998. *Etika Perniagaan Islam, Petaling Jaya:* The International Institute of Islamic Thought, Malaysia.

Bentler, P. M. 1972. A lower-bound method for the dimension-free measurement of internal consistency. *Social Science Research* 1: 343-357.

Bettencourt, L. A., Gwinner, K.P. & Meuter, M. L. 2001. A comparison of attitude, personality, and knowledge predictors of service-oriented organizational citizenship behaviors. *Journal of Applied Psychology* 86(1): 29-41.

Beugre, C. D. 1998. *Managing fairness in organizations.* Westport, CT: Greenwood Publishing Incorporated

Beugre, C. D. 2005. Understanding injustice-related aggression in organization: A cognitive model constant. *International Journal of Human Resource Management* 16(7): 1120-1136.

Bies, R. J., Christopher, L., Martin, & Brockner, J. 1993. Just laid off, but still a "good citizens?" Only if the process is fair. *Employee Responsibilities and Rights Journal* 5(3): 227-239.

Bies, R. J. & Moag, J. F. 1986. Interactional justice: communication criteria of fairness. In R. J. Lewiciki, B. H. Sheppard, & M. H. Bazerman (Eds.), *Research on negotiation in organization* (Vol. 1, pp. 43-55) Greenwich, CT: JAI Press.

Blau, P. 1964. Exchange and power in social life. New York: Wiley. Brayfield, A. H. & Rothe, H. F. (1951).An index of job satisfaction. *Journal of Applied Psychology* 35: 307-311.

Blood, M. R. 1969. Work values and job satisfaction. *Journal of Applied Psychology* 53(6): 456-459.

Bolat, O. I. 2010. The relationship between leader-member exchange and organizational justice in hotels. *European Journal of Economics, Finance, and Administrative Science* 26: 115-125.

Bontis, N., Lorne D. Booker, L. D. & Serenko, A. 2007. The mediating effect of organizational reputation on customer loyalty and service recommendation in the banking industry. *Management Decision* 45(9):1426-1445.

Borman, W. C. 2004. The concept of organizational citizenship. *Personal Decisions Research Institutes* 13(6): 238-241.

Borman, W. C. & Motowidlo, S. J. 1993. Expanding the criterion domain to include element of contextual performance. In N. Schmitt & W. C. Borman (Eds.) *Personnel selection in organization* (pp. 71-98). San Francisco: Jossey – Bass.

Brewer, M.B. 2004. Taking the social origins of human nature seriously. *Personality and Social Psychology* 8(20): 107-113.

Brief, A. P. & Aldag, R. J. 1994. The study of work values: A call for a more balanced perspective, in Borg. I, and Mohler, P.P. (Eds.) *Trends and perspective in Empirical Social Research*, De Gruyter, New York: 99-124.

Brief, A. P. & Motowidlo, S. J. 1986. Prosocial organizational behaviors. *Academy of Management Review* 11: 710-725.

Brockner, J., Siegel, P. A., Daly, J. P., Tyler, T. & Martin, C. 1997. When trust matters: The moderating effect of outcome favourability. *Administrative Science Quarterly* 42(3): 558-584.

Byrne, Z. S. & Cropanzano, R. 2001. To which source do I attribute this fairness? Differential effects of multiple – foci justice on organizational work behaviors. Paper presented at 15th annual conference of the Society of Industrial and Organizational Psychology, New Orleans, L.A.

Cardona, P., Lawrence, B.S. & Bentler, P.M. 2004. The influence of social and work exchange relationship on OC. *Group and Organization Management* 29: 219-247.

Cherrington, D. 1980. *The Work Ethic: Working Values and Values that Work.* AMACOM, New York, NY.

Cho, J. & Kessler, S. R. 2008. Employees' distributive justice perceptions and organizational citizenship behaviors: A social exchange perspective. *International Academy of Business and Econo*mics 8(6): 131-137.

Chu, C., Lee, M. S., Hsu, H. M. & Chen, C. 2005. Clarification of antecedents of hospital nurse organizational citizenship behavior- an example from Taiwan regional hospital. *Journal of Nursing Research* 13(4): 313-323.

Coate, N. 1987.The Confucian ethic and spirit of Japanese capitalism. *Leadership and Organization and Development Journal* 8: 17-22.

Cohen, A. & Vigoda, E. 2000. Do good citizen make good organizational citizens? An empirical examination of the relationship between general citizenship and organizational citizenship behaviors in Israel. *Administrative and Society* 32(5): 596-625.

Cohen-Charash, Y. C. & Spector, P. E. 2001. The role of justice in organizations: A Meta–analysis. *Organizational Behavior and Human Decision Processes* 86(2): 278-321.

Colquitt, J. A. 2001. On the Dimensionality of Organizational Justice: A Construct Validation of a Measure. *Journal of Applied psychology* 86: 386-400.

Colquitt, J.A., Conlon, D.E., Wesson, M.J., Porter, C.O.L.H. & Ng, Y.K. 2001. Justice at the millennium: A meta-analytic review of 25 years of organizational justice research. *Journal of Applied Psychology* 86 (3): 425–445.

Colquitt, J. A. & Greenberg, J. 2003. *Organizational justice: A fair assessment of the state of the literature.* Organizational Behavior the statue of the science. Manwan, NJ: Erlbaum.

Colquitt, J. A., LePine, J. A. & Wesson, M. J. 2009. *Organizational behavior: improving performance and commitment in workplace.* McGraw-Hill Irwin, New York.

Colquitt, J. A., Noe, R. A. & Jackson, C. L. 2002. Justice in teams: Antecedents and consequences of procedural justice climate. *Personnel Psychology* 55(1): 83-109.

Colquitt, J. A, Scott, B. A., Judge, T. A. & Shaw, J. C. 2006. Justice and personality: Using integrative theories to derive moderators of justice effects. *Organizational Behavior and Human Decision Processes* 100(1): 110-127.

Colquitt, J. A. & Shaw 2005. How should organizational justice be measured? In J. Greenberg & J. A. Collquitt (Eds.) *The handbook of organizational justice* (pp 113-152). Mahwah, NJ: Erlbaum.

Congleton, R. 1991. The economic role of a work ethic. *Journal of Economic Behavior and Organization* 15(3) 365-385.

Cooper, D. R. & Schindler, P. S. 2003. *Business research methods* (8th Eds.). New York: McGraw Hill Irwin.

Cowherd, D. M. & Levine, D. I. 1992. Product quality and pay equity between lower level employees and top management: An investigation of distributive justice theory. *Administrative Science Quarterly* 37: 302-320.

Cropanzano, R. & Ambrose, M. L. 2001. Procedural and distributive justice is more similar than you think: A monistic perspective and a research agenda. In J. Greenberg & R. Cropanzano (Eds.), *Advance in organizational justice* (pp. 119-151) Stanford, CA: Stanford University Press.

Cropanzano, R., Bowen, D. E. & Gilliland, W. 2009. The management of organizational justice. *Academy of Management Journal.* November: 34-48.

Cropanzano, R., Byrne, Z., Bobcel, D. R. & Rupp, D. 2001. Moral virtues, fairness heuristics, social entities and other denizens of organizational justice. *Journal of Vocational Behavior* 58: 164- 209.

Cropanzano, R. & Greenberg, J. 1997. Progress in organizational justice: tunneling through the maze. In C. Cooper & I. Robrtson (Eds), *International review of industrial and organizational psychology* (pp. 317-372). New York: Wiley.

Cropanzano, R. & Mitchell, M. S. 2005. Social exchange theory: An interdisciplinary review. *Journal of Management* 31: 874-900.

Cropanzano, R., Prehar, C. & Chen, P. Y. 2002.Using social exchange theory to distinguish procedural justice from interactional justice. *Group and Organizational Management* 27: 324-351.

Dannhauser, Z. 2007. *Can positive impact of servant leaders be associated with behaviors paralleling followers' success*: Virginia Beach, VA: Regent University, School of Global Leadership and Entrepreneurship.

Dar, H. A. & Presley, J. R. 1999. Islamic finance: A Western perspective. *International Journal of Islamic Financial Services* 1(1): 1 – 9.

Davis, M. H. 1980. *A multidimensional approach to individual differences in empathy.* JSAS Catalog of Selected Documents in Psychology, 10: 85.

Department of Statistics Malaysia 2010. In MCMC. 2010 http://www.statistics.gov.my/portal/index.php?option=com_content&view=article&id=363&Itemid=149&lang=en#8 [17 March 2013].

Edwards, J. R. 2001. Multidimensional constructs in organizational behaviour research: An integrative analytical framework. *Organizational Research Methods* 4(2): 144-192.

Eisenberger, R., Huntington, R., Hutchison, S. & Sowa, D. 1986. Perceived organizational support. *Journal of Applied Psychology* 71:500-507.

Elovainio, M., Kivima, K. M. & Helkama, K. 2001.Organizational justice evaluations, job control, and occupational strain. *Journal of Applied Psychology* 86:418–424.

Esposito, J. L. 2005. *Islam: The straight path.* New York: Oxford University Press.

Eroglu, S. G. 2009. A study of organizational justice perception and job satisfaction. Pamukkale University School of Social Science Master's Thesis, Ontario, pp. 1- 223.

Farāhī, Majmū'ah Tafāsīr, 2nd ed. (Faran Foundation, 1998), 347.

Farh, J. L., Early, P. C. & Lin, S. 1997. Impetus for action: A cultural analysis of justice and organizational behavior in Chinese society. *Administrative of Science Quarterly* 42: 421- 444.

Farh, J. L., Podsakoff, P. M. & Organ, D. W. 1990. Accounting for organizational citizenship behaviors: Leader fairness and task scope versus satisfaction. *Journal of Management* 16: 705-722.

Farh, J. L., Zhong, C. B. & Organ D. W. 2004.Organizational citizenship behavior in the people's republic of china. *Organization Science* 15(2): 2004.

Fassina, N. E., Jones, D. A. & Uggerslev, K. L. 2008. Meta- analytic tests of relationships between organizational justice and citizenship behaviour: Testing agent-system and shared-variance models. *Journal of Organizational Behaviour* 29: 805-828.

Fay, B., 1996. *Contemporary philosophy of social science*, Blackwell, Oxford.

Fehr, E. & Fischbacher, U. 2003. The nature of human altruism.*Nature* 425: 785-791.

Fischer, R. & Smith, P. B. 2006. Who cares about justice? The moderating effect of values on the link between organizational justice and work behaviour. *Applied Psychology: An International Review* 55(4): 541-562.

Folger, R. & Cropanzano, R. 1998. *Organizational justice and human resource management.* Thousand Oaks, CA: Sage.

Folger, R. & Greenberg, J. 1985. Procedural justice: Interpersonal behavior as exchange. In K. M. Rowland and G. R. Ferris (Eds), *Research in Personal and Human Resource Management* 3: 141-183.

Folger, R. & Konovsky, M. A. 1989. Effects of procedural and distributive justice on reaction to pay raise decision. *Academy of Management Journal* 32: 115-130.

Fox, S., Spector, P. E. & Miles, D. 2001. Counterproductive work behavior (CWB) in response to job stressors and organizational justice: Some mediator and moderator tests for autonomy and emotions. *Journal of Vocational Behavior* 59: 291-309.

Furnham, A. 1987. Work related beliefs and human values. *Personality and Individual Difference* 8: 627-637.

Furnham, A. 1990. *The protestant work ethic.* London: Routledge.

Gadot, E. V., Beeri, I., Shemesh, T. B. & Somech, A. 2007. Group- level organizational citizenship behavior in the education system: A scale reconstruction and validation. *Education Administration Quarterly* 43(4): 462-493.

Gait, A. & Worthington, A. 2007. An empirical survey of individual consumer, business firm and financial Institution, attitudes towards Islamic Methods of Finance.University of Wollongong, School of Accounting and Finance Working Paper Series No. 07/08.

George, J. M. 1990. Personality, affect, and behavior in groups. *Journal of Applied psychology* 75: 107-116.

George, J. M. 1991. State or trait: Effect of positive mood on prosocial behaviors at work. *Journal of Applied psychology* 76: 299-307.

George, J. M. & Battenhausen, K. 1990. Understanding prosocial behavior, sales performance, and turnover: A group-level analysis in a service context. *Journal of Applied psychology* 75(6): 698-709.

George, J. M., & Brief, A. P. 1992. Feeling good- doing good: A conceptual analysis of the mood at work–organizational spontaneity relationship. *Psychological Bulletin* 112: 310-329.

George, J. M. & Jones, G. R. 1997. Organizational spontaneity in context. *Human Performance* 10: 153-170.

Gibb, H. A. R., Karmers, J. H., Levi-Provencal, E., & Schacht, J. (eds.). 1979. Akhlak. *In Encyclopedia of Islam* (New end., vol. 1, p.325). Leiden: E. J. Brill.

Gibbs, P., Ilkan, M. & Pouloukas, S. 2007. The ethics of marketing in Muslim and Christian communities. *Equal Opportunities International* 26(7): 678-92.

Goles, T. & Hirschheim, R. 2000. The paradigm is dead, the paradigm is dead... long live the paradigm: The legacy of Burrell and Morgan. *Omega* 28: 249-268.

Goulding, C. 1999. Consumer research, interpretive paradigms and methodological and ambiguities.*European Journal of Marketing* 33(9/10): 859-87.

Gouldner, A. W. 1960. The norm of reciprocity. *American Social Review* 25: 161-178.

Graham, J. W. 1986. Principled organizational dissent.A theoretical essay. In B. M. Staw & L. L. Cummings (Eds.), *Research in Organizational Behavior* 8: 1-52. Greenwich, CT: JAI Press.

Graham, J. W. 1989. Organizational citizenship behavior: Construct redefinition, operationalization, and validation. Unpublished working paper. Loyola University of Chicago.

Grant, A. M. & Mayer, D. M. 2009. Good soldiers and good actors: Prosocial and impression management motives as interactive predictors of affiliative citizenship behaviors. *Journal of Applied Psychology* 94: 900–912.

Green, P. E. & Rao, V. R. 1970. Rating scales and information recovery – how many scales and response categories to use? *Journal of Marketing* 34:33-39.

Greenberg, J. 1987. *A taxonomy of organizational justice the*ories. Academy of Management, Sage, Thousand Oaks, CA.

Greenberg, J. 1990a. Organizational justice: Yesterday, today and tomorrow. *Journal of Management* 16: 399-432.

Greenberg, J. 1990b. Employee theft as a reaction to underpayment inequity: The hidden costs of pay cuts. *Journal of Applied Psychology* 75: 561-568.

Greenberg, J. 1993. Justice and organizational citizenship: A commentary on the state of the science. *Employee Responsibilities and Rights Journal* 6(3): 249-256.

Greenberg, J. 2001. Setting the justice agenda: seven unanswered question about "what, why, and how". *Journal of Vocational Behaviors* 58: 210-219.

Greenberg, J. 2006. Losing sleep over organizational injustice: Attenuating insomniac reaction to underpayment inequity with supervisory training in interactional justice. *Journal of Applied Psychology* 91: 58-69.

Greenberg, J. & Colquitt, J. A. 2005. *Handbook of organizational justice.* Mahwah, NJ: Erlbaum.

Greenberg, J. & Folger, R. 1983. Procedural justice, participation and the fair process effect in groups and organizations. In P. B. Paulus (Ed.), *Basic group process* (pp.235-256) New York: Springer- Verlag.

Harlos, K. P. & Pinder, C. C. 2000. Emotions and injustice in the workplace. In S. Fineman (Ed.), *Emotion in organizations* (Vol. 2, pp. 255-276).

Hauenstein, N. M. T., McGonigle, T. & Flinder, S.W. 2001. A meta-analysis of the relationship between procedural justice and distributive justice: Implications for justice research. *Employee Responsibilities and Rights Journal* 13: 39-56.

Hellriegel, D., Jackson, S.E., Slocum, J. Straude, G. Amos, T., Klopper, H.B., Louw, L & Oosthuizen, T. 2001. *Management.*South Africa. Oxford University Press.

Helm, S. Eggert, A. & Garnefeld, I. 2010. Modeling the impact of corporate reputation on customer satisfaction and loyalty using partial least squares, In V. Esposito Vinzi, W.W. Chin, J. Henseler & H. Wang (Eds.) *Handbook of partial least squares*, Heidelberg: Springer.

Hemdi, M. A. & Nasurdin, A. M. 2008. Investigating the influence of organizational justice on hotel employees' organizational citizenship behavior and turnover intentions. *Journal of Human Resource in Hospitality Tourism* 7: 1-23.

Henry, C. M. & Wilson, R. 2004. *The politics of Islamic finance.* Edinburgh University Press, Edinburgh.

Hitt, W. 1990. *Ethics and leadership: Putting theory into practice.* Columbus: Battle Memorial Institute.

Hoffman, B. J., Blair, C. A., J. P. & Woehr, D. J. 2007. Expanding the criterion domain? A quantitative review of the OCB literature. *Journal of Applied Psychology* 92: 555–566.

Hofstede, G. 1980. *Culture's consequences: International differences in work-related values.* Beverly Hills CA: Sage Publications.

Hofstede, G. 1999. Problems Remain, but theories will Change: The universal and the specific in 21st- century global management. *Organizational Dynamics* 18: 34–45.

Holmbeck, G. N. 1997. Toward terminological, conceptual, and statistical clarity in the study of mediators and moderators: Examples from the child-clinical and pediatric psychology literatures. *Journal of Consulting and Clinical Psychology* 4: 599–610.

Holtz. B. C. & Harold, C. M. 2009. Fair today, fair tomorrow? A longitudinal investigation of overall justice perceptions. 2009. *Journal of Applied Psychology* 94(5): 1185-1199.

Homans, G. C. 1974. *Social behavior: its elementary forms,* rev. ed. New York: Harcourt, Brace, Jovanovich.

Hunt, S. D. & Vitell, S. J. 1986. A general theory of marketing ethics. *Journal of Micromark* 6: 5-15.

Huseman, R. C., Hatifield, J. D. & Miles, E. W. 1987. A new perspective on equity theory: the equity sensitivity construct. *Academy of Management Review* 12: 222-234.

Ibn Kaldun, A-R. 1989. *The Maqaddimah: An introduction to history*. Princeton University Press, Princeton, NJ (trans. By Franz Rosenthal & edited by N. J. Dawood).

Ibn-Kather 2000. *Tafsir Ibn-Kather*. *Riyadh*: Darussalam Publishers & Distributers.

IIies, R., Nahrgang, J. D. & Morgeson, F. P. 2007. Leader member exchange and citizenship behaviors: Ameta-analysis. *Journal of Applied Psychology* 92: 269-277.

Ikhwan-us-safa 1999. *Letters of Ikhwan-us-Safa*, Vol. 1, Dar Sader, Beirut.

Ince, M. & Gul, H. 2011. The role of organizational communication on employee's perception of justice: A sample of public institution from turkey. *European Journal of Social Sciences* 21(1): 106-124.

Iqbal, Z. 1997. Islamic Financial System. *Finance and Development* 34(2): 42-45.

Iqbal, Z. & Mirakhor, A. 2007. *An introduction to Islamic finance: Theory and practice*, John Wiley and Sons Ltd, Chichester.

Iqbal, Z. & Molyneux, P. 2005. *Thirty years of Islamic banking: History, performance and prospect*. Palgrave Macmillan, New York, NY.

IOSCO Islamic Capital Market Task Force 2012. http://www.cmda.gov.mv/docs/Islamic%20Finance%20Terms.pdf [8 April 2012]

Islamic-Dictionary.com 2012. http://www.islamic-dictionary.com/index.php?word=%28saw%29 [8 April 2012].

Islamic-Dictionary.com 2012. http://www.islamic-dictionary.com/index.php?word=aqeedah [8 April 2012].

Islamic-Dictionary.com 2012. http://www.islamic-dictionary.com/index.php?word=%28swt%29 [8 April 2012].

Islamic-Dictionary.com 2012. http://www.islamic-dictionary.com/index.php?word=Ibadah [8 April 2012]

Islamic-Dictionary.com 2012.
http://www.islamic-dictionary.com/index.php?word=%28ra%29 [8 April 2012].

Islamic-Dictionary.com 2012.
http://www.islamic-dictionary.com/index.php?word=quran [10 April 2012].

Islamic-Dictionary.com 2012.
http://www.islamic-dictionary.com/index.php?word=Shariah [10 April 2012].

Islamic-Dictionary.com 2012.
http://www.islamic-dictionary.com/index.php?word=Sunnah [10 April, 2012].

Islamic-Dictionary.com 2012.
http://www.islamic-dictionary.com/index.php?word=jibraeel [10 April, 2012].

Jabatan Perdana Menteri 2010. Positioning financial services as the bedrock of the high-income economy. *In economic transformation programme: A roadmap for Malaysia* (Chapter 7), pp.209-252. http://etp.pemandu.gov.my/upload/etp_handbook_chapter_7_financial_sevices.pdf.

James, D. 1993. The social context of organizational justice: Cultural, intergroup, and structural effects on justice behaviors and perceptions. In R. Cropanzano (Ed.), *Justice in the workplace: Approaching fairness in human resource management* (pp. 21-50). Hillsdale, NJ: Erlbaum Associates.

Jawahar, I. M. & Carr, D. 2007. Conscientiousness and contextual performance: The compensatory effects of perceived organizational support and leader-member exchange. *Journal of Management Psychology* 22(4): 330-349.

Mohammad, J., Quoquab, F., & Alias. M. 2010. Organizational justice and organizational citizenship behavior in higher education institution. *Global Business and Management Research: An International Journal* 2(1): 13-32.

Mohammad, J., Quoquab, F. & Alias, M. 2011. Job satisfaction and organizational citizenship behaviour: An empirical study at higher learning institutions. *Asian Academy of Management Journal* 16(2): 149:165.

Johansson, J. K. & Yip, G. S. 1994. Exploiting globalization potential: U.S. and Japanese strategies. *Strategic Management Journal* 15(8): 579– 601.

Jones, D. A. & Martens, M. L. 2009. The mediating role of overall fairness and the moderating role of trust certainty in justice-criteria relationships: the formation and use of fairness heuristics in the workplace. *Journal of Organizational Behaviour* 30: 1025-1051.

Jones, H. B. J. 1997. The Protestant ethic: Weber's model and the empirical literature. *Human Relations* 50(7): 757-778.

Joy, V. L. & Witt, L. A. 1992. Dely of gratification as a moderator of the procedural justice and distributive justice relationship. *Group and Organization Management* 17: 297-308.

Junaidah Hashim. 2008. The Quran-based human resource management and its effects on organizational justice, job satisfaction and turnover intention. *The Journal of International Management Studies* 3(2): 148-159.

Kahf, M. 1999. Islamic banks at the threshold of the third millennium. *Thunderbird International Business Review* 41(4/5): 445-460.

Kamdar, D., McAllister, D. J. & Turban, D.B. 2006. All in a day's work: How follower individual differences and justice perception predict OCB role definition and behavior. *Journal of Applied Psychology* 91(4): 841:855.

Kamdar, D. & Van Dyne, L. 2007. The joint effects of personality and workplace social exchange relation-ships in predicting task performance and citizenship performance. *Journal of Applied Psychology* 92 (5):1286–1298.

Karambayya, R. 1990. Contexts for organizational citizenship behavior: Do high performing and satisfying units have better citizens? Unpublished manuscript, New York University.

Karriker, J. & Williams, M. 2009. Organizational justice and organizational citizenship behavior: A mediating multifoci model. *Journal of Management* 35(1):112-135.

Katz, D. 1964. The motivational basis of behavior. *Behavioral Science* 9(2): 131- 156.

Kelley, T. l. 1927. *Interpretation of educational measurments*. Yonkers, New York: World Book Company.

Khalil, M. & Abu-Saad, I. 2009.Islamic work ethic among Arab college students in Israel. *Cross Cultural Management: An International Journal* 16(4): 333-346.

Khan, K., Abbas, M., Gul, A., & Raja, U. (2013). Organizational justice and job outcomes: Moderating role of Islamic work ethic. Journal of Business Ethics, 117 (1), 1-12.

Khan, M. M. & Bhatti, M. I. 2008. Islamic banking and finance: On its way to globalization. *Managerial finance* 34(10): 708-725.

Khir, K., Gupta, L. & Shanmugam B. 2008. *Islamic banking: A practical perspective*. Kuala Lumpur: Pearson Malaysia Sdn.Bhd.

Khraim, H. S. 1999. Religiosity, socioeconomic status, ethnic intensity and Malay consumer behavior. Unpublished thesis, School of Management, USM.

Khurshid Ahmad 2002. *Islam: Its meaning and message*. Kuala Lumpur: Islamic Book Trust.

Kickul, J. & Lester, S. W. 2001. Broken promises: equity sensitivity as a moderator between psychological contract breach and employee attitudes and behaviour. *Journal of Business and Psychology* 16(2): 191-217.

Kidron, A. 1978. Work values and organizational commitment. *Academy of Management Journal* 21(2): 239-247.

Kim, K. & Frazier, G. L. 1997. Measurement of distributor commitment in industrial channels of distribution. *Journal of Business Research* 40(2): 139-154.

Kim, T. Y. & Leung, K. 2007. Forming and reacting to overall fairness: a cross –cultural comparison. *Organizational Behaviour and Human Decision Process 104: 83-95.*

Kirkman, B. L., Lowe, K. B. & Gibson, C. B. 2006. A quarter century of Culture's consequences: A review of empirical research incorporating Hofstede's cultural values framework. *Journal of International Business Studies* 37: 285–320.

Klendauer, R. & Deller, 2009. Organizational justice and managerial commitment in corporate mergers. *Journal of Management Psychology* 24(1): 29-45.

Koh, H. C. & Boo, E. H. Y. 2004. Organizational ethics and employee satisfaction and commitment. *Management Decision* 42(5): 677-693.

Konovsky, M. A. & Folger, R. 1991. The effect of procedural and distributive justice on organizational citizenship behavior. Unpublished manuscript, A. B. Freeman School of Business, Tulane University.

Konovsky, M. A. & Organ, D. W. 1996. Dispositional and contextual determinates of organizational citizenship behavior. *Journal of Organizational Behavior* 17:253-266.

Konovsky, M. A. & Pugh, S. D. 1994. Citizenship behavior and social exchange. *Academy of Management Journal* 37(3): 656-669.

Korsgaard, M. A., Meglino, B. M., Lester, S.W. & Jeong, S. S. 2010. Paying you back or Paying me forward, understanding rewarded and unrewarded OCB. *Journal of Applied Psychology* 95(20): 227-290.

Koster, F. & Sanders, K. 2006. Organizational citizens or reciprocal relationships? An empirical comparison. *Personnel Review* 35(5): 519-537.

Koys, D. J. & DeCotiis, T. A. 1991. Inductive measures of psychological climate. *Human Relations* 44(3): 265-276.

Krishnan, V.R. & Arora, P. 2008. Determinants of transformational leadership and organizational citizenship behavior. *Asia Pacific Business Review* 4(1): 34-43.

Kumar, K., Bakhshi, A. & Rani, E. 2009. Linking the 'Big Five' personality domains to organizational citizenship behavior. *International Journal of Psychological Studies* 1(2): 73-81.

Kutcher, E. J., Bragger, J. D., Srednicki, O. R. & Masco, J. L. 2010. The role of religiosity in stress, job attitudes, and organizational citizenship behavior. *Journal of Business Ethics* 95: 319-337.

Lambert, E. G., Tolar, T. C., Pasupuleti, S., Hall, D. E. & Jenkins, M. 2005. The impact of distributive and procedural justice on social service workers. *Social Justice Research* 18(4): 411-427.

LaFree, G. 1999. Declining violent crime rates in the 1990s: Predicting crime booms and busts. *Annual Review of Sociology* 50(6): 317-332.

Lavelle, J.J., Brockner, J., Konovsky, M. A., Price, K. H., Henley, A. B., Taneja, A. & Vinekar, V. 2009. Commitment, procedural fairness, and organizational citizenship behavior: A multifoci analysis. *Journal of Organizational Behavior* 30:337-357.

Law, K. S., Wong, C. S. & Mobley, W. H. 1998. Toward taxonomy of multidimensional constructs. *Academy of Management Journal Review* 23:742-755.

Lee, K. & Allen, N. J. 2002. Organizational citizenship behavior and workplace deviance: The role of affect and cognitions. *Journal of Applied Psychology* 87(1): 131-142.

LePine, J. A., Erez, A. & Johnson, D. E. 2002. The nature and dimensionality of organizational citizenship behavior: A critical review and meta-analysis. *Journal of Applied Psychology* 87(1): 52-65.

Lester, S. W., Meglino, B. M. & Korsgaard, M. A. 2008. The role of other orientation on organizational citizenship behavior. *Journal of Organizational Behavior* 29: 829-841.

Leventhal, G. S. 1980. What should be done with equity theory? New approaches to the study of fairness in social relationships. In K. J. Gergen, M. S. Greenber & R. H. Willis (Eds.), *Social Exchange: Advances in Theory and Research*, New York: Plenum Press.

Lin, C. P., Lyau, N. M., Tasi, Y. H., Chen, W. Y. & Chiu, C. K. 2010. Modeling corporate citizenship and its relationship with organizational citizenship behaviors. *Journal of Business Ethics* 95:357-372.

Lind, E. A. 2001a. Fairness heuristic theory: justice judgments as pivotal cognitions in organizational relations. In J. Greenberg & R. Cropanzano (Eds), *Advance in organizational justice* (pp. 56-88). Stanford, CA: Stanford University Press.

Lind, E. A. 2001b. Thinking critically about justice judgments. *Journal of Vocational Behavior* 58: 220-226.

Lind, E. A. & Tyler, T. 1988. *The social psychology of procedural justice*, Penum, New York: Plenum Press.

Lindley, P. & Walker, S. N. 1993. Theoretical and methodological differentiation of moderation and mediation. *Nursing Research* 42: 276–279.

Lipset, S. 1990. The work ethic-then and now. *Public Interest* 98: 61-69.

Lohmöller, J.-B. 1989. *Latent variable path modeling with partial least squares.* Heidelberg: Physica-Verlag.

Lovell, S.E., Anton, J., Mason, C. & Davidson, A. 1999. Does Gender affect the Link between Organizational Justice and Organizational Citizenship Behavior and Performance Evaluation? *Sex Roles* 41(5/6): 469-478.

Lum, L., Kervin, J., Clark, K., Reid, F. & Sirole, W. 1998. Exploring nursing turnover intent: Job satisfaction, pay satisfaction, or organizational commitment? *Journal of Organizational Behaviour* 19: 305-320.

MacKenzie, S. B., PodasKoff, P. M. & Fetter, R. 1991.Organizational citizenship behavior and objective productivity as determinants as salesperson's performance. *Organizational Behavior and Human Decision Process* 50:123-150.

MacKenzie, S. B., PodasKoff, P. M. & Fetter, R. 1993. The impact of organizational citizenship behavior on evaluations of salesperson performance. *Journal of Marketing* 57: 70-80.

Malaysia Pew Forum, 2010. The Future of the Global Muslim Population. http://features.pewforum.org/muslim-population-graphic/#/Malaysia. [10 January 2012]

Marimuthu, M, Jing, C. W., Gie, L. P., Mun, L. P. & Ping T. Y. 2010. Islamic banking: Selection criteria and implications. *Global Journal of Human Social Science* 52(10): 52-62.

Marjoribanks, M. 1998. Factors affecting the self-concepts of South African students. *Journal of Social Psychology* 138 (5): 572-580.

Mason, C. M. & Griffin, M. A. 2002. Group task satisfaction-applying the construct of job satisfaction to groups. *Small Group Research* 33(3): 271-312.

Masterson, S.S., Lewis, K., Goldman, B.M. & Taylor, M.S. 2000. Integrating justice and social exchange: The differing effect of fair work procedures and treatment on work relationships. *Academy of Management Journal* 43: 738-748.

McCain, S. L., Tsai, H. & Bellino, N. 2010. Organizational justice, employees' ethical behavior, and job satisfaction in the casino industry. *International Journal of Contemporary Hospitality Management* 22(7): 992-1009.

McDowall, A. & Fletcher, C. 2004. Employee development: An organizational justice perspective. *Personnel Review* 33: 8-29.

McNeely, B. L. & Meglino, B. M. 1994. The role of dispositional and situational antecedents in prosocial organizational behavior: an examination of the intended beneficiaries of prosocial behavior. *Journal of Applied Psychology* 79: 836-844.

Meglino, B. M. & Korsgaard, M. A. 2004. Considering rational self-interest as disposition: Organizational implications of other orientation. *Journal of Applied Psychology* 89: 946-959.

Meglino, B. M. & Korsgaard, M. A. 2006. Considering situational and dispositional approaches to rational self-interest: An extension and response to De Dreu. *Journal of Applied Psychology* 91: 1253-1259.

Merrens, M.R. & Garrett, J. B. 1975.The Protestant ethic scale as a predictor of repetitive work performance. *Journal of Applied Psychology* 60: 125-127.

Metwally, M. 2006. Economic consequences of applying Islamic principles in Muslim societies. *Journal of Islamic Banking and Finance* 23(1):11-33.

Miller, D. T. 1999. The norm of self-interested. *American Psychologist* 54: 1053-1060.

Mitrano, J. R. 1997. That's not fair: The social construction of organizational (in) justice among professionals. *Sociological Inquiry* 67: 182-206.

Mohammad Akram Laldin 2008. Islamic financial system: The Malaysian experience and the way forward. *Humanomics* 21(3): 217-238.

Mohd.Bakir Mansor. 2008. Misunderstandings in Islamic banks. In ISDEV's Lecture Seri IV. Training Room, Institute Post-Graduate Studies, Universiti Sains Malaysia. 14th May 2008.

Mohd. Rosmizi Abd Rahman 2010. *Introduction to Islamic and Buddhist personal ethics*. University Sains Islam Malaysia Publisher. Negeri Sembilan, Malaysia.

Zulkifli Muhammad, Azleen Liias, Mohd Fahmi Ghazali, Rosita Chong Abdullah & Hanudin 2008. An analysis of Islamic ethics in Islam and medium enterprises (SMEs). *Unitare E-Journal* 4(1):46-58.

Mohsen N. R. 2007. Leadership from the Qura'an operationalization of concepts and empirical analysis: Relationship between taqwa, trust, and business leadership effectiveness. Thesis submitted for the fulfillment of the requirements for the degree of Doctoral of Philosophy, University science Malaysia.

Moon, H., Kamdar, D., Mayer, D. & Takeuchi, R. 2008. Me or we: The role of personality and justice as other-centered antecedents of innovative citizenship behaviour within organization. *Journal of Applied Psychology* 93(1): 84-94.

Moorman R. H. 1991. The relationship between organizational justice and organizational citizenship behaviors: Do fairness perceptions influence employee citizenship? *Journal of Applied Psychology* 76 (6): 845- 855.

Moorman, R. H. 1999. Perceived organizational support and the meaning of just procedures: Sorting the relative contribution of POS and procedural justice in predicting organizational citizenship behaviour. Presented at the 14th Annual Conference of the Society of Industrial and Organizational Psychology in Atlanta, G. A.

Moorman, R.H. & Blakely, G. L. 1995. Individualism-collectivism as an individual difference predictor of organizational citizenship behavior. *Journal of Organizational Behavior* 16: 127-142.

Moorman, R. H. Blakely, G. L. & Niehoff, B. P. 1998. Does perceived organizational support mediate the relationship between procedural justice and organizational citizenship behavior. *Academy of Management Journal* 41(3): 351- 357.

Moorman, R. H., Niehoff, B. P. & Organ, D. W. 1993. Treating employees fairly and organizational citizenship behavior: Sorting the effects of job satisfaction, organizational commitment, and procedural justice. *Employee Responsibilities and Rights Journal* 6(3): 209-225.

Morgeson, F. P. 1999. Understanding prosocial constructs in organizational behavior theory and research: Toward a role theory conceptualization. Paper presented at the annual meeting of the Academy of management, Chicago.

Morrison, E. W. 1994. Role definitions and organizational citizenship behavior: The importance of employees' perspective. *Academy of Management Journal* 37: 1543-1567.

Morrison, E. W. & Phelps, C. C. 1999. Taking charge at work: extra role efforts to initiate workplace change. *Academy of Management Journal* 42: 403-419.

Motowidlo, S. J. 2000. Some basic issues related to contextual performance and organizational citizenship behavior in human resource management. *Human Resource Management Review* 10(1): 115-126.

Motowidlo, S. J., Borman, W. C. & Schmit, M. J. 1997. A theory of individual differences in task and contextual performance. *Human Performance* 10: 71-83.

Motowidlo, S. J. & Schmit, M. J. 1999. Perfomance assessment in uniqe jobs. In D. R. Ilgen & E. D. Pulakos (ED.), *the changing nature of performance* (pp. 56-86). San Francisco: Jossey-Bass.

Motowidlo, S. J. & Van Scotter, R. 1994. Evidence that task performance should be distinguished from contextual performance. *Journal of Applied Psychology* 79(4): 475-480.

Muchinsky, P. M. 2000. *Psychology applied to work: An introduction to industrial and organizational psychology (6ᵗʰed),* Belmont, CA: Wadsworth/ Thomas Learning. 275-284.

Ahmad, M. S. 2011. Work ethics: An Islamic Prospective. *International Journal of Human Sciences* 8(1): 850-859.

Munene, J. C. 1995. "Not–on-seat" an investigation of some correlates of organizational citizenship behavior in Nigeria, *Applied Psychology: An International Review* 44:111-122.

Myers, M.D. 1997. Qualitative research in information systems. *MIS Quarterly* 21:241-242.

Naresh Kumar & Raduan Che Rose.2009. Examining the link between Islamic work ethic and innovation capability. *Journal of Management Development* 29(1): 79-93.

Naser, S. H. 1984. Islamic work ethics. *Hamdard Islamicus* 7(4): 25-35.

Near, J. P. & Miceli, M. P. 1987. Whistle-blowers in organizations: Dissidents or reformers? In L. L. Cummings & B. M. Staw (Eds.*) Research in organizational behavior* (9: 321-368). Greenwich, CT: JAI Press.

Nemeth, C. J. & Staw, B. M. 1989. The tradeoffs of social control and innovation in small groups and organizations. In L. Berkowitz (Ed.), *Advances in experimental social psychology* 22:175–210.New York: Academic Press.

Neuman, G. A. & Kickul, J. R. 1998. Organizational citizenship behavior: Achievement orientation and personality. *Journal of Business and Psychology* 13: 263-279.

Niehoff, B. P. & Moorman, W. V. 1993. Justice as a mediator of the relationship between methods of monitoring and organizational citizenship behavior. *Academy of Management Journal* 36(3): 527-556.

Nik Mu'tasim Abdul Rahman, 2001. Multidimensional approach to the study of organizational commitment: Empirical evidence from Malaysia context. Unpublished thesis submitted in the fulfillment of the degree of Doctor of philosophy at the University of Strahclyde.

Nik Mu'tasim Ab Rahman, Nordin Muhamad, & Abdullah Sanusi Othman. 2006. The relationship between Islamic work ethics and organizational commitment: A case analysis. *Malaysian Management Review* 41(1):79-89.

Noe, R. A., Hollenberck, J. R., Gerhart, B. & Wright, P. M. 2000. *Human resource management: Gaining a competitive advantage.* Boston: Irvin McGraw-Hill Higher Education.

Norlela Kamaluddin & Siti Khadijah Manan 2010. The conceptual framework of Islamic work ethic (IWE). *Malaysian Accounting Review* 9(2): 57-70.

Oliver, N. 1990. Work reward, work values, and organizational commitment in an employee-owned firm: evidence from the UK. *Human Relations* 43(6): 513 526.

Organ, D. W. 1988a. *Organizational citizenship behavior: The good solider syndrome.* Lexington, MA: Lexington Books.

Organ, D. W. 1988b. A restatement of the satisfaction-performance hypothesis. *Journal of Management,* 14: 547-557.

Organ, D. W. 1990. The Motivational basis of Organizational Citizenship Behavior. *Research in Organizational Behavior* 12: 43-72.

Organ, D. W. 1994. Personality and organizational citizenship behavior. *Journal of Management* 20: 465-478.

Organ, D. W. 1997. Organizational citizenship behavior: It's construct clean-up time. *Human Performance* 10(2): 85-97.

Organ, D. w. & Konovsky, M. 1989. Cognitive versus affective determinants of organizational citizenship behavior. *Journal of Applied Psychology* 74: 157-164.

Organ, D. W. & Lingle, K. 1995.A meta-analytic review of attitudinal and dispositional predictors of organizational citizenship behavior. *Personnel Psychology* 48: 775-802.

Organ, D. W. & Paine, J. B 1999. A new kind of performance for industrial and organizational psychology: Resent contributions to the study of organizational citizenship behavior. *International Review of Industrial and Organizational Psychology* 14: 337-368.

Organ, D. W., Podaskoff, P. M. & Mackenzie, S. B. 2006. *Organizational citizenship behavior: its nature, antecedents, and consequences.* Thousand Oaks, CA: Sage publication.

Organ, D. W. & Ryan, K. 1995. A meta-analytic review of attitudinal and dispositional predictors of organizational citizenship behavior. *Personal Psychology* 48(4): 775-802.

Orvis, K. A., Dudely, N. M. & Cortine, J. M. 2008. Conscientiousness and reactions to psychological contract breach: A longitudinal field study. *Journal of Applied Psychology* 93(5): 1183-1193.

Yunus, O. M., Abdul Rahim, A., Shabuddin, A., & azlan, M. Work ethic of Malaysian civil servants. *Proceedings of 2nd international conference on business and economic research (2nd ICBER 2011).* Holiday Villa Beach Resort and Spa, Langkawi Kedah, Malaysia. 14-16 March 2011

Penner, L. A., Dovidio, J.F., Piliavin, J.A. & Schroeder, D.A. 2005. Prosocial behavior, multilevel perspectives. *Annual Review of Psychology* 56: 365-392.

Penner, L. A., Midili, A. R. & Kegelmeyer, J. 1997. Beyond job attitudes: A personality and social psychology perspective on the cases of organizational citizenship behavior. *Human Performance* 10(2): 111-131.

Pillai, R., Schreisheim, C.A. & Williams, E.S. 1999. Fairness perceptions and trust as mediators for transformational and transactional leadership: A two-sample study. *Journal of Management* 25: 897-933.

Podaskoff, P. M., Aherne, M. & MacKenzie, S. B. 1997.Organizational citizenship behavior and quantity and quality of workgroup performance. *Journal of Applied Psychology* 82(2): 262- 270.

Podaskoff, P. M. & Mackenzie, S. B. 1992. An empirical examination of the effect of organizational citizenship behaviors (OCBs) on organizational success: Do OCBs help or hinder organizational performance? Paper presented at Academy of Management Meeting, Las Vegas.

Podaskoff, P. M. & MacKenzie, S. B. 1994. Organizational citizenship behavior and sales unit effectiveness. *Journal of Marketing Research* 31: 259-298.

Podaskoff, P. M. & MacKenzie, S. B. 1997. The impact of organizational citizenship behaviors on organizational performance: A review and suggests for future research. *Human performance* 10(2): 133- 151.

Podaskoff, P. M., MacKenzie, S. B. & Hui, C. 1993. Organizational citizenship behaviors as determinates of managerial evaluations of employee performance: A review and suggestion for future research. In G. R. Ferris & K. M. Rowland (EDs), *Research in personnel and human resource management*, 11: 1-40. Greenwich, CT: JAI.

Podaskoff, P. M., MacKenzie, S. B., Lee, J. Y. & Podaskoff, N. P. 2003. Common method biases in behavioral research: A critical review of the literature and recommended remedies. *Journal of Applied Psychology* 88: 879-903.

Podaskoff, P. M., MacKenzie, S. B., Paine, J. B. & Bachrach, D. G. 2000. Organizational citizenship behavior: A critical review of the theoretical and empirical literature and suggestion for future research. *Journal of Management* 26(3): 513- 563.

Podaskoff, P. N., Whiting, S. W., Podaskoff, P. M. & Blume, B. D. 2009. Individual- and organizational –level consequences of organizational citizenship behaviors: A meta-analysis. *Journal of Applied Psychology* 94(1): 122-141.

Pond, S. B., Nacoste, R. W., Mohr, M. F. & Rodriguez, C. M. 1997. The measurement of organizational citizenship behavior: Are we assuming too much? *Journal of Applied Social Psychology* 27: 1527-1544.

Puffer, S. M. 1987. Prosocial behavior, noncompliant behavior, and work performance among commission sales people. *Journal of Applied Psychology* 72: 615-621.

Putti, J. M., Aryee, S. & Liang, T.K. 1989. Work values and organizational commitment: A study in the Asian context. *Human Relations* 42(3): 275-288.

Raja, U., Johns, G. & Ntalianis, F. 2004. The impact of personality on psychological contracts. *Academy of Managements Journal* 47(3): 350-367.

Ramayah, T., Lee, J. W. C. & Chyaw, J. B. 2011. Networking collaboration and performance in the tourism sector. *Service Business* 5: 411-428.

Randall, D. & Cote, J. 1991. Interrelationships of work commitment constructs. *Work and Occupations* 18(2): 194-211.

Rasinski, K. A. 1987. What is fair or is it? Value differences underlying public views about social justice. *Journal of Personality and Social Psychology.* 53: 201-211.

Reason, P. & Rowan, J. 1981. *Human Enquiry: A Sourcebook in New Paradigm Research.* Chichester: Wiley.

Reaves, C. C. 1992. *Quantitative research for the behavioural science.* John Wiley & Sons, Inc. New York.

Rego, A. & Cunha, M. P. E. 2008. Organizational citizenship behaviors and effectiveness: An empirical study in two small insurance companies. *The Service Industry Journal* 28(4): 541-554.

Rego, A. & Cunha, M. P. E. 2010. Organizational justice and citizenship behaviour: A study in the Portuguese cultural context. *Applied Psychology: An International Review* 59(3): 404-430.

Rego, A., Riberiro, N. & Cunha, M. P. 2009. Perception of organizational virtuousness and happiness as predictors of organizational citizenship behaviors. *Journal of Business Ethic* 93: 215-235.

Rice, G. 1999. Islamic ethics and the implications for business. *Journal of Business Ethics* 18(4): 345-358.

Roscoe, J. T. 1975. *Fundamental research statistics for the behavioral science* (2nded.). New York: Holt, Rinehart and Winston.

Rotundo, M. & Sackett, P. R. 2002. The relative importance of task, citizenship, and counterproductive performance to global rating of job performance. A policy- capturing approach. *Journal of Applied Psychology* 87: 66-80.

Rushton, J.P. 1984. The altruistic personality: Evidence from laboratory. In E. Staab, D., Bar-Tal J. Kerylowski, and J. Reykowski (Eds) *Development and Maintenance of Prosocial Behaviour: International Perspectives on Positive Morality,* New York: Plenum Press: 271-290.

Ryan, J. L. 2002. Work values and organizational citizenship behaviors: Values that work for employees and organization. *Journal of Business and Psychology* 17(1): 123-132.

Saeed, K. 1997. A comparison: the Islamic economic system. http://www.pak. econmist.com/database1/97/97/-33-8.htm [9 June 2010].

Saeed, M., Ahmed, Z. U. & Mukhtar, S. 2001. International marketing ethics from an Islamic Perspective: A value-maximization approach. *Journal of Business Ethics* 32: 127–142.

Samad, A. 2004. Performance of interest-free Islamic banks vis-à-vis interest-based conventional banks of Bahrain. *IIUM Journal of Economics and Management* 12(2): 1-15.

Schaik, D. V. 2001. Islamic banking. *The Arab Banking Review* 3(1): 45-52.

Schappe, S. P. 1998. The influence of job satisfaction, organizational commitment, and fairness perceptions on organizational citizenship behavior. *The Journal of Psychology* 132(3): 277-290.

Sharma, J. p., Bajpai, N., & Holani, U. 2011. Organizational citizenship behavior in public and private sector and its impact on job satisfaction: A comparative study in Indian perspective. *International Journal of Business and Management* 6(1): 67-75.

Schminke, M., Amborse, M. L. & Noel, T. W. 1997.The effect of ethical frameworks on perceptions of organizational justice. *Academy of Management Journal* 40: 1190-1207.

Schnake, M. 1991. Organizational citizenship: A review proposed model and research agenda. *Human Relation* 44: 735-759.

Scholl, R. W., Cooper, E. A. & Mckenna, J. F. 1987. Referent selection in determining equity perceptions: Differential effects on behavioral and attitudinal outcomes. *Personnel Psychology* 40:1130124.

Scott, P. A. & Colquitt, J. A. 2007. Are organizational justice effect bounded by individual differences? An examination of equity sensitivity, exchange ideology, and the big five. *Group and Organization Management* 32(3): 290-325.

Shadish, w. r. & Sweeney, r. b. 1991. Mediators and moderators in meta-analysis: There's a reason we don't let dodo birds tell us which psychotherapies should have prizes. *Journal of Consulting and Clinical Psychology* 59(6): 883-893.

Shapiro, D. 2001. The death of justice theory is likely if theorists neglect the wheels already invented and the voices of the injustice victims. *Journal of Vocational Behaviour* 58: 235-242.

Shapiro, S.S. & Wilk, M.B. 1965.An analysis of variance test for normality (complete samples).*Biometrika* 52 (3/4): 591-611.

Shaw, M. E. & Wright, J. M. 1967. *Scale for measurement of attitudes.* New York: McGraw-Hill.

Sheehy, J. W. 1990. New work ethic is frightening. *Personal Journal* 69(6)28-36.

Sheppard, B. H., Lewicki, R. J. & Minton, J. W. 1992. *Organizational justice: The search for fairness in the workplace.* New York: Lexington Books.

Shimko, B. W. 1992. Pre-hire assessment of the New York force: Finding wheat (and work ethic) among the chaff. *Business Horizons* (May–June): 60–65.

Shweta & Jha, S. 2009. Determinants of organizational citizenship behavior: A review of literature. *Journal of Management and Public Policy* 1(1): 33-42.

Siddiqui, S. H. 2001. Islamic Banking: True Modes of Financing. *New Horizon* 109 (May-June).

Simon, H. A. 1990. A mechanism for social selection and successful altruism. *Science* 250: 1665-1668.

Simon, H. A. 1993. Altruism and economics. *American Economic Review* 83: 156-161.

Smeesters, D., Wheeler, S.C. & Kay, A. C. 2009. The role of interpersonal perception in the prime-to-behaviors pathway. *Journal of Personality and Social Psychology* 96(2): 395-414.

Smith, C.A., Organ, D.W. & Near, J. P. 1983. Organizational citizenship behavior: Its nature and antecedents. *Journal of Applied Psychology* 68: 653-663.

Smith, P.C., Budzeika, K. A., Edwards, N. A., Johnson, S. M & Bearse, L. N. 1986. Guidelines for clean data: Detection of common mistakes. *Journal of Applied Psychology* 71(3): 457-460.

Sobh, R. & Perry, C. 2006. Research design and data analysis in realism research. *European Journal of Marketing* 40(11/12): 1194-1209.

Soper, D.S. 2013. A-priori Sample Size Calculator for Structural Equation Models [Software]. http://www.danielsoper.com/statcalc [20 January 2013].

Sparrow, P.R. 2006. International management: Some key challenges for industrial and organizational psychology. *International Review of Industrial and Organizational Psychology* 21: 189-266.

Sparrow, P. R., Chadrakumara, A. & Perera, N. 2010. Impact of work values and ethics on citizenship and task performance in local and foreign invested firms: A test in a developing country context. 11th International Human Resource Management Conference (pp 1-25). Birmingham, UK: Aston Business School.

Sparrow, P.R. & Wu, P. 1998. How much do National value orientations really matter? Predicting HRM preferences of Taiwanese employees. *Employee Relations* 20(1): 26-56.

Spitzmuller, M., Van Dyne, L. & Ilies, R. 2008. *Organizational citizenship behaviour: A review and extension of its nomological network.* Baring: Organizational Behavior (Handbook). Page: 106-123.

Staufenbiel, T. 2000. Antecedents and consequences of voluntary work engagement. *Gruppendynamik – Zeitchrift fur Angewandte Sozialpsycologie* 31(2) 169-183.

Sudin Haron, S. 1999. *Islamic banking rules and regulations.* Pelanduk Publication. Kuala Lumpur.

Sudin Haron, Norafifah Ahmad & Sandra, L. P. 1994. Bank patronage factors of Muslim and non-Muslim customers. *International Journal of Bank Marketing* 12(1): 32-40.

Sudin Haron & Wan Nursofiza Wan Azmi 2008. Determinants of Islamic and conventional deposits in the Malaysian banking system. *Managerial Finance* 34(9): 618-643.

Tadajewski, M. 2006. Remembering motivation research: Toward an alternative genealogy of interpretive consumer research. *Marketing Theory* 6(4): 429-466.

Tansky, J. W. 1993. Justice and organizational citizenship behaviour: What is the relationship? *Employee Responsibilities and Rights Journal* 6: 195-207.

Tekleab, A., Takeuchi, R. & Taylor, A. G. 2005. Extending the chain of the relationships among organizational justice, social exchange, and employee reactions: The role of contract violations. *Academy of Management Journal* 48(1): 146-157.

Tepper, B. J. 2001. Health consequences of organizational injustice: Test of main and interactive effect. *Organizational Behaviour and Human Decision Processes* 86: 197-215.

Tepper, B. J. & Taylor, E. C. 2003. Organizational citizenship relationship among supervisors and subordinates procedural justice perceptions and behaviours. *Academy of Management* 40: 82-111.

Terry, D.J., Hogg, M.A. & White, K.M. 1999. The theory of planned behaviour: Self-identity, social identity and group norms. *British Journal of Social Psychology* 38: 225-244.

Thibaut, J. & Walker, L. 1975. *Procedural justice: A psychological analysis.* Hillsdale, NJ: Lawrence Erlbaum Associates.

The Asian banker 2012. The global Islamic largest banks. http://www.theasianbanker.com/bankmetrics/ab500/2011-2012/the-global-islamic-largest-banks [18 march 2012].

The Encyclopedia of World Religions. 1998. Cited in Abd Rahman, M. R. 2010. *Introduction to Islamic and Buddhist personal ethics.* University Sains Islam Malaysia Publisher. Negeri Sembilan, Malaysia.

The Future of the Global Muslim Population.Malaysia Pew Forum 2010. http://en.wikipedia.org/wiki/Islam_in_Malaysia (8 April 2012).

The pew forum on religion and public life 2010. The future of global Muslim population. http://features.pewforum.org/muslim-population-graphic/#/Malaysia [6 Jun 2013].

The World Book Encyclopedia. 1993. Vol. 6. London: World Book.

Thibaut, J. & Walker, L. 1975. *Procedural justice: A psychological analysis.* Hillsdale, NJ: Lawrence Erlbaum Associates.

Tinker, T. 2004. The enlightenment and its discontents: Antinomies of Christianity, Islam and the calculative sciences.*Accounting, Auditing & Accountability Journal* 17(3): 442-475.

Tornblom, K. Y. & Vermunt, R. 1999. An integrative perspective on social justice: Distributive and procedural fairness evaluations of positive and negative outcome allocation. *Social Justice Research* 12: 39-64.

Turnipseed, D. L. 2002. Are good soldiers good? Exploring the link between organizational citizenship behaviour and personal ethics. *Journal of Business Research* 55: 1-15.

Turnipseed, D. L. & Murkison, E. C. 1996. Organizational citizenship behabior: An examination of the influence of workplace. *Leadership and Organization Development Journal* 17: 42-48.

Tyler, T. R. 1989. The psychology of procedural justice: A test of the group-value model. *Journal of Personality and Social Psychology* 57: 830-838.

Tyler, T. R. & Bies, R. J. 1990. Beyond formal procedures: The interpersonal context of procedural justice. In J. Carroll (Ed.), *Advances in applied social psychology: Business settings* (pp. 77–98). Hillsdale, NJ: Erlbaum.

Tyler, T. R. & Lind, E. A. 1992.A relational mode of authority in groups. In M. P. Zanna (Ed.) *Advance in experimental social psychology* (Vol. 25, pp. 115-191). San Diego, CA: Academic press.

Tyler, T. R., Lind, E. R. & Huo, Y. J. 2000. Cultural values and authority relations: the psychology of conflict resolution across cultures. *Psychology Public Policy and Law* 6: 1138-1163.

Uddin, S. J. 2003. Understanding the framework of business in Islam in an era of globalization: A Review.*Business Ethics: A European Review* 12(1):23-32.

Ushama, T. 1998. *Sciences of Quran*. Kuala Lumpur: International Islamic University Malaysia.

Vaithilingam, S., Nair, M. & Samudra, M. 2006. Key drivers for soundness of the banking sector: lessons for developing countries. *Journal of Global Business and Technology* 2(1): 1- 11.

Van Dyne, L. & Ang. 1998. Organizational citizenship behaviour of contingent workers in Singapore. *Academy of Management Journal* 41: 692-703.

Van Dyne, L., Cummings, L. L. & Parks, L. 1995 Extra-role behaviour: In pursuit of construct and definitional clarity. *Research in Organizational Behaviours* 17: 215- 285.

Van Dyne, L., Graham, J. & Dienesch, R. M. 1994. Organizational citizenship behaviours: Construct redefinition, measurement, and validation. *Academy of Management Journal* 37(4): 765-802.

Van Dyne, L. & LePine, J. 1998. Helping and voice extra-role behaviour: Evidence of construct and predictive validity. *Journal of Management Journal* 41(1): 108- 119.

Van Scotter, J.R. & Motowidlo, S.J. 1996. Inter-personal facilitation and job dedication as separate facets of contextual performance. *Journal of Applied Psychology* 81 (5): 525–531.

Varma, A., Pichler, S., Budhwar, P. & Biswas, S. 2009. Chinese host country nationals'willingness to support expatriates: The role of collectivism, interpersonal affect, and Guanxi. *International Journal of Cross Cultural Management* 9(2):199-216.

Walster, E., Walster, G. W. & Berscheid, E. 1978.*Equity: Theory and research.* Boston: Allyn & Bacon.

Walz, S. M. & Niehoff, B. P. 1996. Organizational citizenship behaviours and their effect on organizational effectiveness in limited menu restaurants. Academy of Management. *Best Paper Proceedings 307-311.*

Wan Norhasniah Wan Husin, W. N. 2012.Work ethics from Islamic perspective in Malaysia. *European Journal of Social Sciences* 29(1): 51-60.

Wanous, J. P. 1974.A causal correlational analysis of the job satisfaction and performance relationship. *Journal of Applied Psychology* 59(1): 134-144.

Warde, I. 2000. *Islamic finance in globally economic.* Edinburgh University Press, Edinburgh.

Weber, M. 1958. *The protestant ethic and the spirit of capitalism*, Charles Scriber's Sons, New York, NY.

Wikipedia. 2011, Islam in Malaysia. http://en.wikipedia.org/wiki/ Islam_in_Malaysia. [9 December 2011]

Williams, J. 2004. Resampling and distribution of the product methods for testing indirect effects in complex models. Unpublished doctoral dissertation, Arizona State University, Tempe, AZ.

Williams, L. J. & Anderson, S. E. 1991. Job Satisfaction and organizational commitment as predictors of organizational citizenship behaviour and in-role behavour. *Journal of Management* 17(3): 601-617.

Williams, S., Pitre, R. & Zainuba, M. 2002. Justice and organizational citizenship behaviour intention: Fair rewards versus fair treatment. *The Journal of Social Psychology* 142(1): 33-44.

Yandle, B. 1992. Does anyone still care? *Supervision* (September): 14–16.

Yousef, D. 2000a.The Islamic work ethic as a mediator of the relationship between locus of control, role conflict and role ambiguity. *Journal of Managerial Psychology* 15(4): 283-302.

Yousef, D. 2000b.Organizational commitment as a mediator of the relationship between Islamic work ethic and attitudes toward organizational change. *Human Relation* 53(4): 513-537.

Yousef, D. 2001. Islamic work ethic: A moderator between organizational commitment and job satisfaction in a cross-cultural context. *Personal Review* 30: 152-169.

Zakari bin Bahari, Z. 2009. The Changes of Product Structure in Islamic Banking: Case Study of Malaysia. Paper presented at Two-Day Conference on Islamic Perspectives on Management and Finance, United Kingdom organized by School of Management, Leicester University, 2-3 July 2009.

Zaharuddin Hj Abd Rahman. 2007. Differences between Islamic Bank and Conventional. *Zaharuddin.net.* http://www.zaharuddin.net/index. php?option=com_content&task=view&id=297&Itemid=72.

Zaher, T. S. & Hassan M. K 2001. A Comparative literature survey of Islamic finance and banking. *Financial Markets, Institutions and Instruments* 10 (4): 155-199.

Zaroug, A. H. 1999. Ethics from an Islamic perspective: basic issues. *The American Journal of Islamic Social Science* 16(3): 45-63.

Zhang, L., Nie, T. & Yongtai, L., 2009. Matching organizational justice with employment modes, strategic human resource management perspective. *Journal of Technology Management in China* 4(2): 180-187.

Appendix

Definitions of The Islamic Termenologies Used in This Book

The present book has utilized several Arabic terminologies that are necessary to discuss the IWEs phenomenon. Definitions of these terminologies are given below.

Allah: Allah (SWT) is the name of the Creator, and the Sustainer of this life and the hereafter (Ibn-Kather 2000).

Akhlaq is the plural of *Kulaq* which refer to innate disposition, charter, behaviour, attitude, custom and tradition (Gibb, Karmers, Levi-Provencal & Schacht 1979)

Aqidah: Refers to the belief system that is based upon a firm conviction in Allah (SWT) and everything related to Him SWT such as, His names and attributes, His angles, His messengers, and His books (Islamic-Dictionary. com 2012).

At-Tirmidhi: is Muhammad ibn `Isa ibn Sura ibn Musa, Abu `Isa al-Sulami al-Tirmidhi. He was a big Islamic scholar and hadith collector and master, and wrote a number of books in history and hadith, among the most famous of which are his five-volume al-Jami` al-kabir, also known as Sahih al-Tirmidhi (Ahlul Bayt Digital Islamic Library Project 2012).

Ayah (Verse): An Arabic word which means sign or evidence that separates the speech before and after, meaning that the Ayah is separate from its previous and subsequent sentence (Ibn-Kather 2000).

Consensus (Ijmaa') and Analogy (Qiyass): These sources are derived from the holy Quran and Hadith means the derivation of a ruling concerning a new situation or problem based on analogy with similar situation dealt with in the Quran and or Hadith.

Gharar: Refers to Islamic finance terminology used to describe risky sale, where details regarding the sale items are uncertain or unknown. Islamic shariah has prohibited this type of financial transaction due to high risk that result from extreme uncertainty (Islamic-Dictionary.com 2012).

Ibadah: It means worship or an act of *ibadah* is an act of worship done for the sake of Allah (SWT) (Islamic-Dictionary.com 2012).

Ijtihad: It refers to the efforts of scholars and jurist to derive and legislate a principles and regulations based on evidence found in the Islamic sources i.e., Quran and the Sunnah.

Iman: Islamic doctrine that refers to the internal part of the religion, and indicates a believer's faith in the metaphysical aspects of Islam. (Farāhī 1998).

Hadith: Documented traditions of the teaching, actions, and sayings of the Prophet Muhammad (saw).

Halal: It represents the things or activities permitted by the *Shariah*.

Haram: It is opposite of *halal* and implies the things or activities prohibited by the Shariah.

(ra): This abbreviation means may Allah be pleased with him or them (Islamic-Dictionary.com 2012).

PBUH: Peace be upon him, is a expression that keen Muslims regularly say after saying (or hearing) the name of any Prophets of Islam (Islamic-Dictionary.com 2012)

Riba': It means interest in which borrower will return to the lender more than the quantity borrowed based on a predetermined percentage. Islamic *Shariah* has forbidden this type of transaction and considered as great sin that should be avoided (Sudin Haron et al. 1994).

Sahih al Bukhari: One the three most trusted collection of hadith along with Sahih Muslim and Muwatta Imama Malik. These Islamic heritage or hadith were collected by the big Muslim scholar Muhammad al Bukhari who was born in 149 A. H. in Bukhara in the territory of Khurasan and died in the year 256 A> H.

SAW: It is an abbreviation of Sallalahu Alaihi Wa-salam which means 'Allah's praise and peace be upon him'. This abbreviation is used after the name of the messenger of Islam Muhammad (SAW) specifically, and it is a form of showing respect. (Islamic-Dictionary.com 2012).

Shariah: Islamic Law concerning the community (Islamic-Dictionary.com 2012).

Surah: It means collection of Ayat (Ibn-Kather 2000).

SWT: Refers to acronym of Subhanahu Wa Ta'ala which means 'Glorious is He and He is Exalted' and it is placed after the name of Allah, as a sign of reverence (Islamic-Dictionary.com 2012). More clearly, it is written in the following way: Allah (SWT).

The Archangel Jibril: It is the Arabic name for the angel of Allah (SWT) (Islamic-Dictionary.com 2012).

The Sunnah: The Sunnah is the ways, teachings and activities of Prophet Muhammad (saw) (Islamic-Dictionary.com 2012).

Printed in the United States
By Bookmasters